Contents

Acknowledgements

The publishers would like to thank both Martin Hewings and Richard Cauldwell, School of English, The University of Birmingham, without whose enthusiasm and assistance the publication of this work, and in particular the recording of the cassette, would not have been possible.

1004093803

The communicative value
of intonation in English

PUBLISHED BY THE PRESS SYNDICATE OF THE UNIVERSITY OF CAMBRIDGE
The Pitt Building, Trumpington Street, Cambridge CB2 1RP, United Kingdom

CAMBRIDGE UNIVERSITY PRESS
The Edinburgh Building, Cambridge CB2 2RU, United Kingdom
40 West 20th Street, New York, NY 10011–4211, USA
10 Stamford Road, Oakleigh, Melbourne 3166, Australia

First published 1997

This book was published in an original version by the University of Birmingham.

Typeset in Swift

A catalogue record for this book is available from the British Library

Library of Congress Cataloguing in Publication data applied for

ISBN 0 521 58587 2 Hardback
ISBN 0 521 58457 4 Paperback
ISBN 0 521 58588 0 Cassette

Transferred to digital printing 2004

Foreword

When David Brazil died in 1995, the lasting influence of his work on intonation had become clear. Discourse Intonation was being cited frequently in scholarly studies and it had been adopted as the basis for teaching intonation in a growing number of English language teaching publications. Two of David Brazil's major books which sought to apply and extend his work were published shortly before his death: *Pronunciation for Advanced Learners of English* (Cambridge University Press, 1994) and *A Grammar of Speech* (Oxford University Press, 1995). As the most detailed statement of the theory of Discourse Intonation is to be found in *The Communicative Value of Intonation in English*, it is timely that this groundbreaking book should now be republished by Cambridge University Press.

David Brazil is perhaps best known for his association with the University of Birmingham, and this began in the mid nineteen sixties. A new degree of Bachelor of Education had been established, and John Sinclair, as Professor of Modern English Language, had insisted that courses on English Language should be a compulsory component of this new degree. This necessitated the retraining of teacher-trainers, and David, then a teacher-trainer, was one of the first to attend lectures on English Language given by John Sinclair and Malcolm Coulthard. There followed a fruitful period of collaboration between these three scholars and others engaged in discourse analysis at the University.

In the early seventies David was seconded to the School of English at the University of Birmingham to conduct research on discourse analysis in projects supported by the Social Science Research Council. It was his work on these projects which became the subject matter of his PhD, and resulted in a number of publications. These included *Discourse Intonation and Language Teaching* (Longman, 1980), co-authored with Malcolm Coulthard and Catherine Johns, and in 1985, *The Communicative Value of Intonation in English*, published as an 'English Language Research Monograph' by the University. By this time, the originality of his work on intonation and the quality of his teaching both in Birmingham and around the world were well recognised.

When *The Communicative Value of Intonation in English* was first written, it was rejected by external publishers on the grounds that it did not 'contribute to the debate'. The debate in question concerned the relationships between intonation and grammar, and intonation and attitudinal meanings. As two of David's starting assumptions in his theory of Discourse Intonation were (a) that intonation choices are not related to grammatical or syntactic categories (rather, they depend on the speaker's contextually referenced perceptions), and (b) that there is no systematic link between intonation and attitude, one can easily see why it was rejected.

However, since its publication the monograph has been a source of inspiration to many students and researchers concerned with the analysis of discourse. This is not the place to list the work which has drawn on David Brazil's ideas. But to give some indication of its variety and breadth, here are some of the topics that students and visiting academics at the University of Birmingham have investigated: intonation in lectures; the English intonation of non-native speakers; the intonation of poems read aloud; intonation in German, Italian, Swedish and Japanese; the intonation of idioms; and the intonation of particular communicative events, such as stories read aloud, radio advertisements, and even shipping forecasts.

Discourse Intonation has also been welcomed by English language teachers as a framework within which they can understand better this complex area of language and develop teaching materials and techniques to convey this to learners. A number of textbooks for teachers have advocated a Discourse Intonation approach, and teaching materials have been published which draw extensively on the description provided in *The Communicative Value of Intonation in English*. These include David's own book, *Pronunciation for Advanced Learners of English*.

One of the attractions of Discourse Intonation to both teachers and researchers is that it provides a manageable tool for analysing and interpreting the intonation choices made by speakers in naturally occurring speech. It is manageable because the description recognises significant intonation choices as being made within a very small number of systems – four in all: *prominence, tone, key* and *termination*. These systems contain a total of thirteen choices, summarised in the following table:

System	Choices	Number
Prominence	prominent/non-prominent syllables	2
Tone	rise-fall, fall, level, rise, rise-fall	5
Key	high, mid, low	3
Termination	high, mid, low	3

The description thus contrasts with others which view intonation as conveying a very large number of attitudinal meanings, or different meanings depending on the grammatical system in which it occurs. Such approaches result in far greater complexity and a potentially open-ended list of meanings attributed to intonation.

For those who are already familiar with other work on intonation *The Communicative Value of Intonation in English* might be seen as presenting an unfamiliar and provocative account. Placed at the centre of the theory are those features of speech that in many other descriptions are seen as peripheral: performance factors and context. However, once the reader is convinced of the validity of David Brazil's starting point, the insights generated by the theory are considerable.

This edition is largely the same as the 1985 original with certain minor amendments. The recording has however been re-done: the original recordings were not made in ideal conditions, and the copying process had led to a deterioration in the masters.

Healthy theories should evolve in the light of what is learned in applying them to real data, and Discourse Intonation is no exception. Although David Brazil was very keen to preserve and promote the essentials of the description, evolution is reflected in his books and papers written since 1985. These, together with his earlier publications, are given in the bibliography at the end of this book.

Martin Hewings
Richard Cauldwell
(School of English, The University of Birmingham)

Preface

This book is about the way intonation affects the communicative value of an English utterance. More simply – and less irritatingly, no doubt – it could be said to be about the meaning of intonation. The problems attendant upon any careful use of the word 'meaning' are very well known, however, and I hope I may be excused for not wanting to engage with them as a preliminary to my main business. My intention in speaking in a loose, pre-theoretical way about something called 'communicative value' is to keep such problems at arm's length, as it were, and leave myself space to work outwards from certain observable facts towards a conceptual framework that brings the operational significance of intonation into a manageable focus.

The first two monographs in the Birmingham *Discourse Analysis* series gave me an opportunity to present some of the main features of an account of the intonation of English which differed from existing accounts in that I sought to make consistent reference to the way speech functions in interactive discourse. More than a decade of work in the area has resulted in considerable elaboration of the schema that was there proposed, and in what I hope I am right in thinking of as refinements of many of the details. What I have attempted here is to summarise the position to which the logic of the earlier work and the careful examination of naturally-occurring data seem both to lead. Much of what was in Monographs I and II will be found to be restated here in some form or other, but restated in a way which relates it to what I believe to be a more satisfactory overall view of intonational meaning.

The wish to display the working of the system *as a whole*, and to show how an appreciation of the workings of its several parts can be mutually illuminating, has, indeed, been one of the bases on which I have made necessary decisions about what to leave out. The other has been the precedence given to consideration of meaning or value of which the title gives warning. I start with the assumption that the first task of the student of intonation is to set up a framework within which the finite set of meaningful oppositions can be identified and characterised, and I seek to do no more than this in a single volume. The reader will find, therefore, that little attention is given to those matters of precise phonetic detail that a book about intonation might be expected to provide.

There are other things for which the reader might look in vain, but for the omission of which I have less clear-cut and principled excuses. They are left out largely to save space, but partly also because of the wish to give a concise and uncluttered statement of a particular view of the phenomenon. The conceptual pattern that informs that view turns out, I think, to be a remarkably simple one, but certain problems attend its explication. I hope my decision to avoid distractions will not be interpreted as ignorance of, or lack of interest in, alternative views.

One thing that is regrettably absent is any indication of how the intonation categories I postulate are *in extenso* in the very large amount of data from which they are, in fact, derived. I can find no more economical way of advancing the exposition than by the use of minimally contrasted pairs, and naturally-occurring speech is not usually a very rich source of these. In point of fact, I have come to realise that there is not quite the worrying incompatibility between research method and presentation method that I once supposed there was. For even when working on real data one is constantly asking what *does* happen and comparing its significance with what (in terms of the evolving description) might *alternatively* have happened. The process of invention seems to be an unavoidable concomitant of observation. The general use of rather short examples may seem to be at odds with my insistence upon the contextual significance of intonational meaning. The reason for using them is not merely that long extracts take up more space than short ones and make the whole organisation of the book more difficult. It is also that the contextual implications of a text become rapidly more complex as the length increases, permitting more and more alternatives. It has generally been thought more helpful to specify the relevant factors in the background to the utterance descriptively, even sometimes anecdotally.

If my method of exposition, which makes use of constructed – and perhaps fanciful – situations, is one of the things that strikes the reader as unusual in a work which has serious theoretical pretensions, another will be the absence of reference to the work of others. This will be noticed in two connections. In the first place there is the large, and growing, body of literature covering the whole field of Discourse Analysis to which I am so obviously indebted. No one familiar with this field will fail to recognise that many of the principles and concepts I invoke in the course of my exposition have their origins somewhere in that literature, though their originators have not usually had intonation specifically in mind. If my book should chance to fall into the hands of the latter, I hope they will excuse my neglect of the normal courtesies. In most cases, I was driven to the decision that simple acknowledgment just would not do, for the genesis of a particular notion in the present description depends often upon an application of another's ideas to which they may well object, and the requisite discussion and justification would have resulted in an impossibly unwieldy book.

Much the same applies to the work of others labouring in the more circumscribed field of intonation. Apart from acknowledging my indebtedness – which I hereby sincerely do – I ought ideally to have shown how my own categories relate to those in other treatments and said why, in each case, I think my own treatment provides the more satisfactory ones. It soon became apparent that the chapter which was to have attempted this would take on the proportions of another book if I was to avoid being overselective or insultingly cursory. Perhaps a brief statement of my position might be acceptable in lieu. There must be a strong expectation that the specific assertions others have made about the 'meaning' of items they use for exemplification will, on the whole, be compatible with any new account. Such assertions represent the considered judgments of scholars and teachers who have acquired an unusual level of sensitivity to the operational significance of intonational phenomena, and one would need seriously to question one's own intuitions if they were very much at odds with theirs. In a sense, they represent a body of informants whom one ignores at one's peril. I count it as evidence in support of the present approach that, provided their judgments are thought of as statements of *local meaning*, there is usually no problem in agreeing to their validity by appeal to the formal oppositions I postulate. There must, after all, be a fair measure of agreement among competent language users about local values: differences lie in the apparatus we need to set up to give generalised expression to the agreement.

Here again, though, a great deal more is involved than a simple point-by-point comparison of different descriptive models. A difficulty facing anyone who undertakes a comparative exercise is the fact that phonologists differ in the assumptions they make about how intonation relates to the other variables language users exploit in pursuit of their manifold communicative ends. Once more a brief statement of my position will have to do duty for the argument I should have liked space to develop. Firstly, I see everything in this book as support for the belief that the conceptual framework we need to capture intonational meaning is freestanding. This is to say that it can be explicated without reference to such other features of the utterance as syntactic descriptions seek to identify. A description which handles intonation properly must, indeed, seek to answer questions of quite a different kind from those which sentence grammars are set up to answer. The latter can be said to start from the assumption that parties to a verbal interaction have available for their use a system for classifying experience which, in theory if not in fact, they share with the whole speech community and which, for most practical purposes, remains constant through time. But to make sense of intonation we need to think of speakers as classifying experience along lines that are valid for themselves and their interactants, and in the here-and-now of the utterance. Each of the oppositions in the meaning system is to be thought of as an occasion for setting up *ad hoc* categories in the light of the speaker's apprehensions of how things presently stand between them and a putative hearer.

To follow this line of thinking further would lead to our asking about the consequences of viewing other aspects of linguistic organisation in the same way. There is certainly reason to think that much of what now gets separated out for special attention under such headings as Syntax, Intonation and Discourse Analysis might be brought to a single focus more satisfactorily than existing sentence-based models have so far achieved. Current orthodoxy postulates a distinction between 'semantics' and 'pragmatics', and is much concerned with where the boundary between them should be drawn. If pragmatics covers that part of the meaning of an utterance that can be explicated only by reference to the including situation, then one option that is certainly open to us is to regard *all* the meaning of normally-used language as a manifestation of pragmatic behaviour. To say this, of course, is to adopt the common-usage sense of the epithet to signify spur-of-the-moment decisions, made in the light of a running assessment of what is desirable to be done and what is the most effective way of achieving it. This is precisely the view of the matter that an examination of intonational phenomena powerfully suggests we should take. And since it seems to be an eminently tenable view of what ordinary conversational practice is like, there must surely be a case for focusing linguistic enquiry upon the mechanisms that make it possible.

I must content myself with simply making this very large claim about the wider implications of what is presented here. Consciousness of those implications has, however, affected my method of exposition in a way which will be obvious to the reader, and which needs a word of explanation. I have tried to be as explicit and precise as possible about the conceptual and theoretical foundations on which each stage of the presentation rests. It may seem perverse to go back to first principles when received terminology and commonly accepted practices are apparently available as shortcuts. If I am guilty of keeping the would-be traveller waiting while I re-invent the wheel, it is because I think the enterprise I have in hand exemplifies in a particularly striking way the general truth that concepts and categories depend for their significance on the model from which they are derived. It is partly to emphasise this that I have adopted the practice of using asterisks to distinguish my own technical terms. These are attached to the first occurrence of the word in the text, the place at which its particular significance is usually stated. For ease of reference, they are then collected into a glossary in Appendix C.

I am indebted to many people for support, help, encouragement and properly critical interest in all that has gone into the genesis and writing of this book. I gratefully plead lack of space once again, this time to excuse myself from trying to name names. Firstly, there are my immediate colleagues in the English Department, and specifically in English Language Research at Birmingham. Then there are the many people who have worked with us in some capacity or other over the last decade. Finally I want to acknowledge the very great profit I have derived from talking about intonation with individuals and groups in so many places in the United Kingdom and abroad. I am aware that much of the original interest that led to these discussions can be traced to the publication of the early monographs. And the generous invitation to once more use this means of disseminating work that is still very much in progress is not the least cause I have to be grateful.

1

A preliminary sketch of the tone unit

Intonation is traditionally equated with variations in the perceived pitch of the speaking voice. We shall begin by examining this characterisation.

Pitch varies continuously from the moment anyone begins speaking to the moment they end. An accurate description of the variation would be exceedingly complex and would reveal nothing of the significantly patterned phenomenon that we take intonation to be. This is because not all the variation has the same kind of communicative significance. The only meaning that the description presented here purports to deal with is of the kind that can be represented as the result of a speaker having made an either/or choice. We are concerned, that is to say, with identifying a set of oppositions* that reside in the language system, knowledge of which we must assume the speaker shares with his/her hearer.

Suppose there is a language system that includes an opposition we can describe in the following terms: having pitched a particular syllable at a certain level, the speaker can, at some subsequent syllable, make a meaningful choice between the same pitch, a higher one or a lower one. Graphically, we might represent the choices at the second syllable thus:

$$
S1 \cdots\!\!-\!\!-\!\!-\!\!\left\{
\begin{array}{l}
S2\ \text{(high)} \\
S2\ \text{(mid)} \\
S2\ \text{(low)}
\end{array}
\right.
$$

Two important conditions are inherent in the kind of situation we have postulated at S2:

(i) if the speaker produces S2 at all he/she cannot avoid choosing one of the three possibilities specified (there is no fourth choice).

(ii) the communicative value of any one choice is defined negatively by reference to the other options available (the value of 'high' is whatever is not meant by 'mid' and 'low' taken together).

This account misses out one very obvious thing we might say about what our speaker does. Having decided, let us say, on a higher choice, he/she must then make a further decision, as to *how much* higher to pitch the syllable. To deal with this kind of decision, any descriptive enterprise would have to concern itself with variation on a continuous scale, and would demand a quite different analytical method from that used here. My aim will be to show that a small set of either/or choices can be identified and related to a set of meaning oppositions that together constitute a distinctive sub-component of the meaning-potential of English.

In accepting this limitation, we are not of course suggesting that variation of the continuous kind has no communicative importance. Individual speakers may well have a predilection for greater or lesser pitch intervals, so that the overall pitch treatment of an utterance will carry a significant component of indexical information; or an increase in anxiety, anger or physical discomfort might result in a gradual rise in the general pitch of the voice: a hearer might, in a given situation, derive a great deal of information of this kind from variation that is superimposed upon the systemically significant changes. Impersonation and similar devices can result in a speaker's deliberately adopting a pitch level or pitch range that is not his/her usual one and the effect is part of the total 'meaning' of his/her present behaviour. None of these effects, or others like them, can be said to be without interest to anyone who wishes to understand how verbal interaction works. But in so far as, say, anger can be attributed to a general rise in pitch, there are theoretically unlimited gradations of 'how high', and so presumably of 'how angry', the speaker may be judged to be. Any attempt to capture the significance of intonation must aim to disentangle, at an early stage, those variations that hearers respond to as pitch placement on a continuous scale and those that they hear and interpret as manifestations of an either/or option. To say this is to adopt a well-established position in linguistics and to assume that it is only phenomena of the latter kind that linguistic techniques are designed to handle. If we re-label the distinction we have made and speak of our object of study as linguistic intonation (as opposed to the other which is non-linguistic) we shall be ascribing to 'linguistic' a definition which probably few people would dispute.

The hypothetical case on which we have based our discussion so far is probably too simple to apply to any real language in at least two ways.

Firstly, we have associated the opposition with a particular syllable. Reality would seem to require that we associate a number of variables globally with a unit that extends over a number of syllables. We shall refer to the stretch of language that carries the systemically-opposed features of intonation as the tone unit*. Our starting assumption will be that hearers are able, on the basis of the overall presentation of the tone unit, to recognise that it carries a number of distinctive intonation characteristics and to differentiate it from otherwise similar tone units having other characteristics. To state what these are, we must make a rough-and-ready reference to what happens at particular syllables, but this practice has to be followed in the awareness that anything affecting physical realisation at one point in the tone unit is likely to affect what happens elsewhere. The several physical features that we find we have to separate out in order to make a usable description occur, in reality, as a complex contour: we may speculate, with some plausibility, that the speaker 'plans' the tone unit and the hearer 'decodes' it *as a whole*. When we say – as expediency compels us to say – that certain speaker-choices are associated with certain syllables, we shall be simplifying to the extent of overlooking this kind of prosodic effect.

The other source of over-simplification is our adherence to the traditional practice of speaking of intonation in terms of pitch variation. It seems inherently improbable that a human being can make systematic variations on one physical parameter without its affecting others. Changes in loudness and in speed result from intimately connected adjustments to the same speech mechanism as that which determines pitch. Isolating any one parameter for attention might well give a quite false notion of what, in the course of ordinary language use, people actually 'hear' when they hear intonation. Instrumental analysis suggests, in fact, that each of the meaningful oppositions our description recognises *can* be identified on the basis of pitch treatment alone. This provides us with a convenient method of characterising the oppositions and enables us to make use of traditional vocabulary like 'high', 'low', 'rise' and 'fall'; we must leave open the possibility that variations other than those in pitch may be of greater operational importance to the language-user in some or even in many cases.

Everything we have said so far in this chapter underlines the need for extreme tentativeness in providing phonetic descriptions of the meaningful choices that make up the intonation system. We have recognised four possible causes of variation between one occurrence of a systemically-meaningful feature and another occurrence of the same feature: it may be overlaid by variation of the continuous, non-systemic, kind; the variables that a description will want to separate out and identify individually may merge into a unified envelope co-terminous with the tone unit; variation on the dimensions of pitch, loudness and time may interact in complex ways as modifications of the segmental composition of the utterance; and idiolectal and dialectal variation may result in a given formal choice having a whole range of different phonetic realisations. To describe a certain intonation feature in such phonetic terms as, for instance, 'high fall' is to take no account of the phonetically distinct events that hearers might classify together as non-significant variants. More seriously, perhaps, it disposes us prematurely to assume that all occurrences of the feature will fit this strictly arbitrary description: in theory we should start with no firm expectation that a particular realisation will necessarily be either a 'fall' or 'high'. A procedure which would seem unlikely to result in an adequate functional description of intonation would be to observe pitch patterns that appear to recur and then to try to ascribe significance to what has been observed. The use of instruments to refine and sophisticate observational techniques would not, in itself, do anything to reverse the directionality of such an exercise. If the same principles are to be applied as have been applied in establishing the set of segmental elements the language employs, then we must start with a hypothesis about meaning: before proceeding to detailed phonetic specification we need to know how many meaningful oppositions there are and how they are deployed with respect to each other within the area of meaning potential that intonation realises.

It is fair to say, of course, that the only research procedure available is to make tentative phonetic observations and try to associate them with generalisable meaning categories. And what applies to the discovery of the meaning system applies equally to its presentation in such a book as this. We have no alternative but to refer to the variables in pseudo-phonetic terms; but we have to stress that such a characterisation is no more than an approximation and a convenience. It is necessary always to preserve a certain distance from the phonetic fact. When we say that there is a 'fall' at a particular point in the utterance, it is not the fact that the pitch falls that we wish to make focal; it is rather the function of the language item which carries it, a function which, as far as we can tell from the examination of a lot of data, is typically realised by a falling pitch.

In practice, the possible discrepancy between meaningful choice and phonetic realisation creates fewer problems than we may have seemed to suggest it will. It must, however, be taken seriously in any description if misunderstanding and misapplication of the categories are to be avoided. For this reason, the sketch of the tone unit that forms the central part of this chapter is presented in such a way as to try to avoid inappropriate precision in describing phonetic realisations. This may seem to the reader to be rather tiresome prevarication. We hope, however, that the prevaricating quotation marks we consistently use with words like 'high' and 'fall' will be accepted as the unavoidable consequences of adopting a proper theoretical position. Only when the set of meaningful oppositions has been described shall we suggest a way of approaching the realisation problem.

Our tone units have some superficial similarities to the entities other descriptions have referred to variously as 'sense groups', 'breath groups' and 'tone groups'. One unresolved issue that these terms reveal is uncertainty about how the observable fact that continuous speech is broken up into perceptible blocks or units is to be interpreted. The labels seem severally to suggest semantic, physiological and formal considerations. There is also uncertainty about how different meaning choices are to be attributed to the analytical unit once it has been identified. Once the boundaries of the unit have been determined, on whatever criteria, the descriptive task has generally been thought to involve identifying sub-components and associating speaker options with each of them. So, for instance, one tradition has categories like 'nucleus', 'pre-head', 'head' and 'tail' and distinguishes different types of each, like 'low pre-head' and 'high pre-head'. A fundamental difference between descriptions is the number of sub-components they recognise and the number of opportunities for speaker-choice they associate with each. The significance of this difference should not be underestimated. By specifying how many possibilities of choice there are in the unit, where they are made, and what relations of interdependence exist among them, the phonologist is making a powerful prediction about what the meaning system is like. If he makes one wrong prediction, he will never achieve a mapping of the descriptive categories into the meaning system.

As we have said, the only procedure that will lead to a model of the meaning system is a lengthy examination of data, during which both ends of the sound-sense continuum are kept in view, and which works gradually towards a matching of intuitively satisfying analyses at both ends. Little purpose would be served by attempting to reconstruct the various stages through which the present description went before it reached the form in which it is presented here. The reader may very reasonably demand that this particular way of analysing the tone unit should be justified: why this way rather than one of the many other ways that the phonetic data would doubtless support? The impossibility of justifying it in advance of the presentation and exemplification of the rest of the description will be apparent from everything we have said. The categories and choices that are here represented are those which are required by a particular view of the meaning system. Their justification is in the extended exposition of that view that constitutes the main part of this book.

The categories of tone unit

It is not difficult to find samples of recorded data in which pauses of some kind segment the stream of speech into units that hearers can readily agree about. At this point we need not enquire further into what, intuitively, is identified for this purpose as a 'pause'. By taking this empirical observation as our starting point, we are emphatically *not* committing ourselves to regarding the pause as criterial. We are simply taking units that do lend themselves to easy identification in this way as specimens of the descriptive category tone unit. Undoubtedly, there are cases where the phonetic evidence for segmentation is less straightforward, and problems of other kinds arise once we move outside a carefully selected corpus. We can, however, reasonably put off confronting such problems until after we have examined some data which, in this particular respect, is easy to deal with:

(1)   // i think on the whole // that these officials // do a remarkably good job // we have to remember // that // they're required // by administrative practice // to take these decisions // on paper // and // most often // when they get these decisions wrong // it's because // they haven't had the opportunity // of talking // face to face // with the claimant // and really finding // the facts //

If we now examine and compare all the segments that this simple transcription procedure recognises, we shall be able to make some preliminary generalisations about the internal organisation of the tone unit.

Firstly, each tone unit has either one or two syllables that a hearer can recognise as being in some sense more emphatic than the others. We shall say that these syllables have prominence*, a feature which distinguishes them from all other syllables. There are two prominent syllables, identified by the use of upper case characters, in each tone unit of the original recorded version of:

> // I think on the WHOLE // that THESE of FICials // do a reMARKably good JOB //

It may seem at first sight that the distribution of prominent syllables is determined by the lexis and grammar of the utterance. For instance, the fact that -mark- rather than any other syllable of *remarkably* is prominent is clearly connected with the way 'stress' or 'accent' is normally associated with this particular syllable in this particular word. There are evidently constraints upon what a speaker may do, but our present concern is to recognise that – such constraints notwithstanding – speakers do have the option of producing alternative versions of some units. The broadcaster might, for instance, have said:

(2)   // i THINK on the WHOLE //

(3)   // do a remarkably GOOD JOB //

(4)   // do a reMARKably GOOD job //

We shall investigate in detail the significance of these variations in the next chapter. Meanwhile we must emphasise that seeing prominence as a feature which speakers can vary voluntarily – seeing that its occurrence is not merely an automatic reflex of other decisions they may have to make of a grammatical and lexical kind – is an essential first step towards grasping its significance as an exponent of part of the meaning system. Of course, we cannot rule out *ab initio* the possibility that otherwise similar utterances that are differentiated only by the incidence of prominence are sometimes in free distribution: that is to say the fact that certain syllables in a tone unit are prominent while others are not might sometimes have no communicative significance. As a matter of principle, however, we shall assume that when a speaker does one thing when he/she could have done another, the decision is in some sense a meaningful one. We shall eventually want to consider how the speaker's freedom of action is limited by constraints of the kind that govern his/her treatment of *remarkably*, but our primary concern is with prominence as an independent variable.

There may not seem to be much scope for plausible redistribution of prominence in these tone units:

|| that THESE of FICials ||

|| MOST OFten ||

It is not difficult, however, to conceive of utterances otherwise similar to these having one prominent syllable instead of two:

(5) || that these of FICials ||

(6) || that THESE officials ||

(7) || most OFten ||

(8) || MOST often ||

The speaker has freedom to vary, not the location, but the number of prominent syllables. Our sample suggests that the latter freedom is limited to assigning *either one or two*. A transcription of the rest of it, indicating all prominent syllables, is as follows:

> || we HAVE to reMEMber || THAT || they're reQUIRED || by
> adMINistrative PRACtice || to TAKE these deCISions || on
> PAper || AND || MOST OFten || when they GET these decisions
> WRONG || it's beCAUSE || they HAVEn't had the
> opporTUNity || of TALKing || FACE to FACE || WITH the
> CLAIMant || and REALly FINDing || the FACTS ||

We can continue to rely upon pre-analytical intuitions to recognise that the syllables we have so far described as prominent are, in reality, of two kinds. To characterise the difference between them, however, we need to go beyond what will be immediately apparent to most hearers. It is best regarded as a difference in the range of meaningful choices associated with the place the syllable occupies. We have already seen that the allocation of prominence is the consequence of a speaker's decision with respect to a binary prominent/non-prominent choice. Additionally, associated with the last prominent syllable in the tone unit but not with any other one, there is a further choice from a set of significant pitch movements or tones*. The syllable, the point of operation of the tone system*, will be referred to as the tonic syllable*. Thus tonic syllables are to be understood as constituting a sub-set of prominent syllables.

The tonic syllables in the first three tone units of our data sample exemplify in succession the tones that are described conveniently in quasi–phonetic terms as the 'fall-rise', the 'rise' and the 'fall':

(9)   WHOLE   of FICials   JOB

In transcriptions, the tonic syllable will be underlined and a symbol will be placed at the beginning of the tone unit to indicate which tone is selected. So in

> // ∨ I think on the WHOLE // ↗ that THESE of FICials // ↘ do a reMARKably good JOB //

the symbols are to be interpreted as meaning 'At the next underlined syllable there is an occurrence of the tone we associate for recognition purposes with a phonetic "fall-rise", "rise" and "fall"'.

These additions to our transcription conventions call for two observations. Firstly, since the tonic syllable is, by definition, the last prominent syllable in the tone unit, underlining it is strictly unnecessary in this piece of data. The need for the convention will become apparent when we come to discuss the question of boundary recognition in later pages. Secondly, the symbols used to represent tones make direct reference to their physical representation. Although it is convenient to use such symbols at this stage, we shall wish to replace them later with others that have functional rather than phonetic connotations, so making it easier to maintain a mental separation between the meaningful decisions the speaker makes and the physical events whereby his decisions are made manifest.

Later tone units in the same sample exemplify the use of a 'level' tone:

(10)   // ⟶ THAT // , // ⟶ AND //

It happens that there are no examples of the fifth option, the 'rise-fall'. The complete set of possibilities comprises:

fall; rise; fall-rise; rise-fall; level

In addition to choosing one of the five tones at the tonic syllable (a choice we have associated with the physical phenomenon, pitch *movement*), the speaker has also to select in a three-term system that we will associate, in a similar provisional and undogmatic way, with the physical fact of pitch level. Retaining our unavoidable concern with phonetic realisation, we can best describe the pitch-level choice by assuming simultaneous choice of a 'falling' tone. While keeping the same pitch movement in // do a reMARKably good JOB // a speaker may vary the height at which the fall begins. What actually happens in our sample will be represented as follows:

(11)   // do a reMARKably good <u>JOB</u> //

This is to be taken to mean that the level at which the falling tone begins is 'low' compared with the level of the preceding prominent syllable *-mark-*. Alternative versions of an otherwise identical tone unit would be:

(12)   // do a reMARKably good <u>JOB</u> // (<u>job</u> falling from 'high' level)

(13)   // do a reMARKably good <u>JOB</u> // (<u>job</u> falling from 'mid' level)

It will be apparent that this set of examples is particularly useful for expository purposes because the tone unit has two prominent syllables, the first of which can be said to be pitched at 'mid' level. In discussing the pitch-level treatment of *job* we have had to be concerned only with relative pitch heights within the tone unit. To generalise the description we have now to consider both how the 'mid' value of *-mark-* is determined and what happens when there is only one prominent syllable in the tone unit.

We shall refer to any prominent syllable like *-mark-* which precedes the tonic syllable in its tone unit as an onset syllable*. (Onset syllables thus constitute another sub-set of prominent syllables and are complementary to tonic syllables.) We have already said that onset syllables, thus defined, differ from tonic syllables in having no pitch-movement choice associated with them: tone is a once-for-all choice for each tone unit. The onset syllable is, however, the place of operation of a separate pitch-level choice, a choice whose communicative significance we shall show to be quite different from the phonetically similar one at the tonic syllable.

Again, without involving ourselves in phonetic detail, we can recognise high, mid and low levels at which the onset may be pitched. The opening three tone units of the extract we are examining will serve to illustrate the differential pitch-level selections at onset and tonic syllables:

$$// ^{\text{I}} \dots \underline{\text{WHOLE}} // \text{THESE} \dots \text{-}\underline{\text{FIC-}} \dots // \dots \text{-MARK-} \dots _{\underline{\text{JOB}}} //$$

All non-prominent syllables have been omitted since these are not relevant to our present concerns. The conventions are to be interpreted as representing the following selections:

> // high onset .. mid tonic // mid onset .. mid tonic // mid onset .. low tonic //

We said earlier that *job* was identified as a low choice by noting its pitch in relation to that of *-mark-* in the same tone unit. In the case of onset syllables, a different diagnostic procedure is followed: comparison is here made with the onset syllable of the previous tone unit. So, *these* is mid because it is lower than *I* (which has already been identified as high); *-mark-* is mid because it is at the same level as *these*.

The expression 'pitch level', and many of the other words we have used in discussing onset and tonic syllables, resembles 'pitch movement' in seeming to refer very positively to the phonetic shape of the utterance. There is an even more immediate need to make a distinction here between physical realisation on the one hand and the meaningful option it realises on the other than there was in the case of tone. A very similar physical feature, namely placing on a three-term system of relative pitch height, serves to realise two quite different options: the significance of pitch level depends upon which of the two syllables we are concerned with. While it is useful to have the term to signify the approximate physical manifestation the two options share, we also need terms which distinguish their functional values. The choice associated with the onset syllable will be referred to as key* and that associated with the tonic syllable as termination*.

It remains to show how the two options are associated with tone units having only one prominent syllable. We can take in such cases by a slight rephrasing of what we said in the last paragraph: key is the choice associated with the first prominent syllable and termination is that associated with the last. If there is no onset syllable, the first prominent syllable is also the last, so there can be no independent choices in the two systems. Selection of a particular pitch level, say high, to realise a term in the key system necessarily involves selection of the corresponding term in the termination system. In

$||$ we ^{HAVE} to $^{re}\underline{MEM}$ber $||$ that they're re$\underline{QUIRED}$ $||$ by adMINistrative $\underline{PRAC}$tice $||$ to TAKE these de$\underline{CIS}$ions $||$ on $\underline{PA}$ per $_{||}$

the pitch level at -quired represents a simultaneous choice of mid key and mid termination, while that at pa- represents selection of the high term in both systems. (It will be necessary, of course, to justify this way of making the analysis by showing that, when there is no onset syllable, the meaning increments derived from the two choices are compatible and both appropriate to the situation.)

Key and termination choices combine freely with all tone choices, so the location of all three may now be represented as follows:

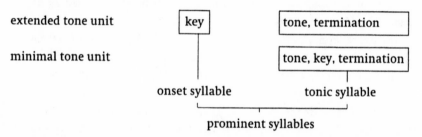

A defining characteristic of the prominent syllable is, then, that it is a decision point in that part of the total pitch treatment of the tone unit that serves to define one or more of the three speaker options we have postulated. It would, of course, be possible to make a phonetic description of the pitch treatment of the non-prominent syllables as well as the prominent ones, but we do not here attribute meaning to the variations that such a description might reveal. It seems that some of them, at least, are not independent of the physical realisations of the three central systems we have described. In so far as this is the case, they are not available to carry separate increments of meaning. It would be rash to deny that some of them might, in fact, make an independent and generalisable contribution to the communicative value of the utterance, but any attempt to describe naturally occurring data must admit to an (at least provisional) circumscription of the phenomena it purports to handle: our present limits are reflected in the transcription conventions we have now introduced. All non-prominent syllables are represented by lower-case letters and placed arbitrarily on the same line as the preceding prominent syllable, except at the beginning of the tone unit when they are placed – equally arbitrarily – on the mid line, thus:

|| AND || MOST OFten || when they GET these decisions
WRONG || it's beCAUSE || they HAVEn't had the
opporTUNity || of TALKing || FACE to FACE || WITH the
CLAIMant || and REALly FINDing || the $_{\text{FACTS}}$ ||

Nothing is implied in this representation about the pitch treatment of non-prominent syllables. Indeed, the latter are only transcribed in order to make the result more readable. If readability is not a consideration, a simplified version can be used:

|| AND || MOST OF- || GET WRONG || -CAUSE || HAVE-
-TUN- || TALK- || FACE FACE || WITH CLAIM- || REAL-
FIND- || $_{\text{FACTS}}$ ||

This last version omits nothing that is relevant to our present concerns.

If we now compare tone units in this way

	I think on the WHOLE	
that	THESE of FIC	ials
do a re	MARKably good JOB	

we can identify a necessary central segment, the tonic segment*, which is delimited by the first and last prominent syllables. Preceding this there may be a proclitic segment*. Following it there may be an enclitic segment*. Using brackets to indicate optional elements, we can represent all tone units thus:

(Proclitic segment) Tonic segment (Enclitic segment)

By definition, neither proclitic nor enclitic segments contain prominent syllables; neither, therefore, is involved in the selectional potentiality of the tone unit. The terms minimal and extended, informally introduced in the earlier diagram can now be applied, more properly, to tonic segments. The tone units we have just compared have extended tonic segments*; those in the following set have minimal tonic segments*:

Proclitic segment	Tonic segment	Enclitic segment
that they're	<u>QUIRED</u>	
on	<u>PA</u>	per
	<u>AND</u>	
the	<u>FACTS</u>	

These examples make it clear that it is the tonic syllable that is the indispensable constituent of the tonic segment, and hence of the tone unit.

The account of the tone unit we have now presented in outline has been based, almost entirely, upon the examination of a mere fragment of data. It remains to consider its general applicability, and in particular to ask what kinds of event outside our minuscule corpus might lead us to consider its categories inadequate.

There are at least three kinds of phenomena that are encountered in some types of data, and that seem not to be easily accommodated in the descriptive apparatus we have to set up.

(i) There may be additional prominent syllables between onset and tonic. We may, for instance, find

(14)   // ＼ do a reMARKably GOOD <u>JOB</u> //

or, if the division into tone units is different

(15)   // ＼ that THESE of FICials do a reMARKably GOOD <u>JOB</u> //

(ii) Stretches of speech bounded by pauses may have no tonic syllable. If the pause is to be regarded as criterial and a tonic syllable an essential constituent, then we have to regard tone units like the first in

(16)   // do a reMARKably // . . . // ＼ GOOD <u>JOB</u> //

as incomplete. (For the difference between this and level tone, see Chapter 9.)

(iii) Conversely, there may be no perceptible boundary within some stretch of speech which, because of the presence of more than one tonic syllable, we should want to regard as more than one tone unit.

Instances of (i) are rare enough in the spontaneous discourse we have examined to suggest that they reflect something special in the circumstances in which they are produced. In Chapter 8 we shall give careful consideration to what those circumstances might be. Meanwhile, we shall proceed on the assumption that even if there are intermediate prominent syllables, this does not affect the validity of anything we have to say about the first and last ones. Consideration of incomplete tone units is also postponed, in this case to Chapter 9. The problem most urgently demanding attention is that presented by the 'phonetically continuous' stretch of speech that has more than one tonic syllable.

The decision to associate no more than one tonic syllable with each tone unit is, of course, a descriptive one. It has been taken, as have all decisions of this kind, in the light of the view of the meaning system that motivates our description. The reason for taking it can be stated very simply: if we have two consecutive and obviously discrete tone units and ascribe communicative value to all the speaker decisions in each of them, then removal of the boundary that divides them does not lead us to revise those values. We cannot demonstrate this in detail until we have gone some considerable way in setting up the meaning system. At this point we will do no more than note the conclusion that attributing significance to an overt boundary, whether realised by a pause or by some other means, is a quite separate matter from attributing significance to the set of speaker-options we have postulated: they should be seen to be separate in the description.

For the phonetician, the least problematical boundaries are, in fact, not those separating tone unit from tone unit but those at which the tonic segment begins and ends. We have already said, as well, that this is the element in which all the significant speaker-decisions are made. Although the three-part account of the tone unit given above is generally satisfactory, and has the advantage of fitting in with some of the more commonly received ideas about segmentation, there are certain stretches of spoken text that invite representation in another way. Non-prominent stretches, which might be transcribed as either enclitic or proclitic segments if there were pauses to determine which, occur rather as continuous 'linking elements' between tonic segments, thus:

> ... tonic segment (linking element) tonic segment (linking element) ...

It will be seen that this representation, which liberates us from the need to find objective criteria for recognising tone unit boundaries, is quite consistent with the model of the meaning system we shall develop.

Our transcription conventions are designed to allow for the omission of the boundary symbol when there seems to be no phonetic justification for introducing one:

(17) $|| \searrow \nearrow$ i DON'T think i <u>CAN</u> come on <u>THURS</u>day $||$

The underlining of *can* and *Thurs-* signifies that there are two tonic syllables and this is sufficient to indicate that there are two tone units. The first tone unit has 'falling' tone, the second 'rising' tone. The absence of an intermediate boundary symbol recognises that we cannot say at what point the enclitic segment of the first ends, and that of the second begins, or whether indeed we should consider that both these elements are present. A transcription that took account only of tonic segments might acknowledge the existence of a notional – but unrealised – break somewhere between *can* and *Thurs-*:

(18) $|| \searrow$ DON'T <u>CAN</u> $|| \nearrow$ <u>THURS</u>- $||$

The marginal significance of the break can best be appreciated by observing the variations that are possible when a speaker, speaking perhaps with marked deliberation, *does* pause perceptibly between tonic segments:

(19) $|| \searrow$ i DON'T think i <u>CAN</u> $|| \nearrow$ come on <u>THURS</u>day $||$

(20) $|| \searrow$ i DON'T think i <u>CAN</u> come $|| \nearrow$ on <u>THURS</u>day $||$

(21) $|| \searrow$ i DON'T think i <u>CAN</u> come on $|| \nearrow$ <u>THURS</u>day $||$

Clearly, it would be highly desirable to include in an account of verbal behaviour an explanation of such variant forms as these. A first step towards doing this – and this is as far as we shall attempt to go in the present book – is to see that they do not affect the value that accrues to the utterance by reason of the choices we have identified in the last few pages.

Prominence and 'stress'

It will be evident that much of what we have taken into account in the definition of the tone unit has been treated in other descriptions under some such heading as 'stress'. Few, if any, treatments of suprasegmental phonology have failed to indicate a relationship between intonation and stress, but the precise nature of this relationship remains an insufficiently examined source of misunderstanding among phonologists. Some attention to the problem is necessary here, if only to make clear what the present book is not concerned with.

Perhaps the least problematical of references to stress are those in dictionaries, where the assignments of 'primary' and 'secondary' stress are taken to be self-evidently justified, even to ordinary dictionary-users who have no kind of phonetic expertise. Examples of dictionary citations which have this amount of information attached are:

> de'cision
>
> ˌcontro'versial

If these words are spoken aloud, simply as *citation forms*, they can be represented, using the conventions set up in the last section, as:

> || de <u>CIS</u> ion ||
>
> || CON tro <u>VER</u> sial ||

Both 'primary' and 'secondary' stress can thus be equated with our *prominence*, the former being distinguished from the latter by the presence of the tone selection. Once we go beyond citation forms, however, we find that the incidence of neither is fully predictable. Characteristically, we encounter forms like:

> a ˌcontroversial de'cision
>
> the deˌcision was contro'versial
>
> ˌvery controversial in'deed
>
> a ˌvery controversial decision in'deed

If these and the two citation forms are brought together, we can discern a very clear pattern:

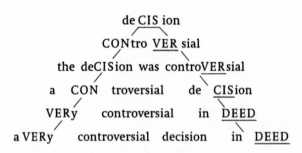

de CIS ion

CONtro VER sial

the deCISion was controVERsial

a CON troversial de CISion

VERy controversial in DEED

a VERy controversial decision in DEED

Some phonologists would want to say that there were 'tertiary' and perhaps other 'degrees of stress' in *con-* and *-ver-* when these happen not to have ' or ₁ ; but to treat 'stress' as a single variable in this way, and to engage in debate as to how many degrees of stress there are, is to overlook two essential facts.

Both are demonstrated by the examples. Firstly, what is called primary or secondary stress has a differential relationship with the word: there is no way of predicting, on the basis of the citation form, whether any syllable will have prominence or not when the word occurs as part of a communicative event. (The fact that we can predict *which* syllable(s) in a word will be prominent if any are is a separate matter.) The allocation of prominence to a word can be shown to be consistently the result of a speaker-decision over and above that which resulted in the choice of the particular lexical item. It is, therefore, independently meaningful. To perceive varying degrees of 'stress' – as people undoubtedly *can* perceive them – is to attend primarily to phonetic differences. The phonologist's task is to identify meaningful contrasts, and in the present context this means distinguishing between features which are word-defining and features which are not. Whatever may be perceived as distinctive about a non-prominent treatment of syllables like *con-* and *-ver-* can be taken to be a simple reflex of some property of the word, not the realisation of a further meaning. A separation has to be made between the observation of what we might provisionally call 'word accent', and the optional superimposition upon 'accented' syllables of choices in the two-term system of prominence.

Further, the treatment of *controversial* in the second and third examples illustrates a common phenomenon which supports a view of the tone unit as in some sense a communicatively functioning whole. Among the many other examples we might cite, we find a similar automatic choice of *which* accented syllable is made prominent in:

|| a University eduCAtion ||

|| he was EDucated at the uniVERsity ||

Very informally, we might say that the precise location of prominent syllables is automatically adjusted to bring them as near the beginning and end of the tonic segment as possible. Note that when the division into tone units is different, we may get a different allocation of prominence, but the same 'rule' applies:

|| it was a VERy controVERsial || deCISion ||

Now what is usually referred to as 'primary stress' in all these examples is the consequence – phonologically speaking – of the superimposition upon the last prominent syllable in the tone unit of a tone choice, *whose meaning attaches to the whole of the tonic segment*. To think of any perceived difference as an opposition between primary and secondary stress is therefore to conflate two kinds of choice, that which affects the meaning-in-discourse of the word (or, as we shall say later, of the *sense* that the word realises) and that which affects the value of the larger unit, the tonic segment.

Saying that there are different 'levels of stress' can be seen, then, as a phonetically motivated comment which actually obscures the fact that the perceived event is the end product of what we can now represent as a three-stage process:

(i) 'Word accents' are an automatic consequence of the assembly of particular lexical items:
    'I shall 'try to 'see 'Tom and 'Mary

(ii) Prominent syllables are next assigned in one of the possible ways (and in accordance with principles to be discussed in the next chapter):
    'i shall TRY to 'see 'tom and MARy
    'i shall 'try to SEE 'tom and 'mary
    etc.

It will be appreciated that neither (i) nor (ii) represents an actual spoken utterance: they are merely indications of the distribution of compulsory accents and the elective allocation of prominent sylla-bles, which can be realised in speech only after the third stage is completed.

(iii) Tone choices are made and attach additional meaning increments to tonic segments:

|| 'i shall TRY || to 'see TOM and MARy ||

|| 'i shall TRY to 'see TOM || AND 'mary || etc.

2

Prominence

Prominence has been characterised as the feature that determines the beginning and end of the tonic segment. It is the incidence of prominence that fixes the domain of the three variables, key, termination and tone. The temporally extensive part of the utterance that is tagged with a meaning increment derived from each of the three systems is limited to the stretch of language that begins with the onset syllable (if there is one) and ends with the tonic syllable. Before going on to consider each of the three systems in turn and to discuss the separate contributions they make to the communicative value of their tone unit, we shall first ask what general significance attaches to a speaker's decision simply to make a particular syllable prominent or non-prominent: that is to say, we shall confine our attention temporarily to the conversational implications of one-by-one occurrences of prominent syllables, leaving for later examination their significance as constituents of tone units.

In practice, it is not easy to attach meaning to syllables at all. The status of the word as the minimal free form in grammar makes it a much more satisfactory focus when one tries to conceptualise the meaningful consequences of the presence or absence of prominence. A description must recognise, at some point, that words may have more than one prominent syllable, but it is better to leave consideration of such cases for a while and proceed as far as we can on the basis of words *having* or *not having* a single prominent syllable. A great deal of harmless simplification is achieved if the descriptive labels 'prominent word' and 'non-prominent word' are adopted as a temporary expedient. By restricting ourselves to the great majority of cases for which this generalisation holds, we can begin by relating the distribution of prominence to an act of selection* in which the speaker is involved.

Selection

Consider the following question/response pair:

(22) Q: What card did you play?
      R: // the QUEEN of HEARTS //

It is easy to see that in the response the word *of* is the only word that could occupy the place between *queen* and *hearts*. If we think of each word as representing a selection from a set of words available at successive places along the time dimension, then at the place filled by *of* there is a set of one. In this respect it can be compared with the place filled by *queen* and *hearts*. If we leave aside for the moment the slightly less straightforward case of *the*, we can show the total range of possibilities thus:

(the)	ace		of	
	two			spades
	.			diamonds
	.			hearts
	queen			clubs
	king			

We will provisionally attribute the fact that *of* is almost certain to be without prominence to its having no selective function: it is the only word that existing circumstances allow. We are here making rather informal use of the notion of a paradigmatic dimension* of language organisation which, with its complementary concept, the syntagmatic dimension*, has been an important part of the model-building apparatus of linguistics, at least since the work of Ferdinand de Saussure (1915). When we speak of a 'paradigm' in a linguistic context, we normally have in mind just such a set of conditions which, residing in the system of the language, reduce the number of items that could fill the third slot in

He wanted / to / find her

to one. The notion we need to invoke at present, however, is importantly different from that captured in the Saussurian characterisation of the paradigm. If we consider each of the slots in 'the queen of hearts', we can see that the speaker has a choice of thirteen and four possibilities at the second and fourth slots respectively; but the limitation has nothing to do with the working of the language system. There is no linguistic reason why the response should not have been 'the prince of forks' or 'the seventeen of rubies' or any of a theoretically unlimited number of combinations. What imposes the limitation is an extralinguistic factor, the conventional composition of the pack of playing cards, with which we must assume both participants are familiar. It is only slightly less obvious that it is the same factor that results in *of* being non-selective. Linguistically, we might have:

	with	
the queen	for	hearts
	etc.	

We shall use the term existential paradigm* for that set of possibilities that a speaker can regard as actually available in a given situation. This will enable us to distinguish it from the general paradigm* which is inherent in the language system. It is clear that at the place occupied by *to* in 'He wanted to find it' the two paradigms coincide: there is no possibility of choice in the existential paradigm because there is none in the general paradigm. In every other slot in our examples, the words comprising the existential paradigm are a sub-set of those comprising the general one. We have to focus now upon some cases where the existential paradigm has only one member.

Consider:

(23)   Q: What heart did you play?   R: // the QUEEN of hearts //

(24)   Q: Which queen did you play?   R: // the queen of HEARTS //

In each of these examples, the question we have provided sets up a context which effectively removes the possibility of choice at one other place. In (23) the person asking the question makes it clear that he/she knows the suit, and in (24) he/she speaks of the denomination as something already known. The respondent's use of *hearts* in the former, and of *queen* in the latter are not the outcome of his/her making any kind of selection, a fact which would probably result, in many circumstances, in their being omitted altogether:

Q: What heart did you play?   R: // the QUEEN //
Q: Which queen did you play?   R: // HEARTS //

It would be a distraction to enquire, at this point, into why speakers might choose to repeat non-selective material. Obviously, the conversational effect is different from that of the minimal response. It is enough to recognise that such repetitions do occur, and that when they do their non-selective value is usually acknowledged by their being made non-prominent.

Once more we shall want to say that what determines the extent of the existential paradigm, reducing it in fact to a set of one, is something additional to the language system. It is because shared understanding with respect to one of the variables has already been acknowledged in the conversation that no selection is involved. We may think, in this particular case, of the wide range of options that comprise the general paradigm at each of the two places being reduced by shared card-playing conventions and then further reduced by shared experience of the immediate conversational environment of the response.

Shared understanding of another kind can be seen to play a part in determining which words are selective and which are not in examples like:

(25)   // TOM dick and HARry //

(26)   // a BOTtle of johnny WALKer //

There is a very strong probability that *Dick* and *Johnny* will lack prominence in real-life occurrences of these tone units. We can connect this with the fact that in the contexts 'Tom . . . and Harry' and 'a bottle of . . . Walker' alternatives scarcely come to mind. Very widely disseminated expectations, which speaker and hearer share, will usually justify treating *Dick* and *Johnny* as non-selective. For a further demonstration of the working of the same mechanism, we can consider:

(27)   Q: Who else have you invited?   R: // JANE sarah and Edith //

This differs from (25) in that the non-selective value of *Sarah* cannot be attributed to culture-wide acquaintance with a particular sequence of names. It is nevertheless the case that the intonation treatment assumes a situation in which, *for the parties involved in the conversation*, mention of the first and last names is enough to eliminate any alternative to the middle one. The three girls may, for instance, be known to be sisters, so that the list, considered as a whole, is existentially synonymous with 'the Robinson children' or 'that lot from number seventeen'. The two examples demonstrate how conversationalists may rely upon shared understandings that have either a very wide currency or a very circumscribed one. Apart from this difference, they show the use of a non-prominent word being motivated in the same way.

Context of interaction

In order to bring together all the examples we introduced into the last section, and also to provide a basis for a further elaboration of the notion of selectivity, it is helpful to set up a theoretical postulate to which we shall apply the term context of interaction*. It is a concept to which we shall need to make constant reference as we discuss the communicative value of each different intonation choice, and successive chapters will require further refinements of it. Initially, we shall consider some of the consequences of a rather self-evident fact: that each tone unit, conceived as a further increment in the stream of speech, occurs at a specific time and place. The here-and-now of utterance provides for each tone unit a unique conversational setting. One feature of this setting is the peculiar understanding then existing between speaker and hearer.

Some features of that understanding are virtually permanent. A shared awareness of what the language system allows can, for instance, be assumed to be a feature of the context of interaction when both participants are mature speakers of the language: as we have seen, constraints inherent in the general paradigm are to be thought of as always binding upon the existential one. What makes the setting unique, however, is the fact that, after each step forward along the time continuum, it includes shared awareness of what has been said before. The state of understanding comprises to some extent the very long-standing elements and to some extent newly-created, and perhaps never-to-be-repeated, elements that originate in the unfolding discourse. Between these two extremes there may of course be other relevant considerations of greater or lesser durability. Certain understandings develop cumulatively during the course of successive conversations. Familiarity with some matter of topical concern may result in a meshing of minds that will last as long, but only as long, as it remains topical.

But there is also another sense in which the context of interaction for each tone unit is unique. Cross-cutting the continuum we have imagined between the longstanding and ephemeral bases of understanding, there is a difference of another kind. Our examples have shown that the existential paradigm is sometimes affected by familiarity with some well-known idiom or trade-name, a familiarity we can safely attribute to a large, culturally-defined group. Probably the group that shares a working command of the language-system will be greater. On the other hand, knowledge of the composition of the family next door is likely to be accessible to a comparatively small number of people. We must recognise too, the rather important limiting case where factors affecting understanding are accessible to no-one except the participants.

There is no need to dwell upon the multitude of factors that determine the socially-constructed and ever-changing background against which each new development in a conversational encounter occurs. We can think of it as originating in the interpenetrating life-histories of the parties concerned. In so far as these interpenetrate the biographies of others, we may find features in the context of interaction that have wider currency, extending sometimes to a membership of an entire speech community or cultural group. But we must be prepared also to find speakers acting on the basis of understandings that are accessible to no-one but themselves. In so far as the relevant factors include a shared awareness of the ongoing encounter, we may hope to reconstruct the context of interaction by examining some record of the 'text' of the encounter. But as analysts we cannot hope to make sense of a speaker's behaviour unless we are willing to take into account very much more than is vested with the comparative objectivity of a transcribed text. Indeed, the implication in all this that, in some ideal instance, the context of interaction might be objectively verified is probably less than helpful, as we shall now try to show.

Projection

The method of exposition we have adopted so far in this chapter is open to misinterpretation in at least one important respect. To make our point about the relationship between the intonational treatment of an utterance and the context of interaction, we have made an explicit characterisation of the latter our starting point. We have represented the item upon whose intonation we have wanted to focus as occurring subsequently to some other event or events: in examples like (22) it has followed a question; in others, we have declared that some kind of understanding was previously established. The view we have encouraged is one of the speaker matching his/her utterance to a context of interaction which he/she finds ready-made as it were. We must now alter the perspective in order to take into account the active and independent part he/she can play in any conversational proceedings.

Communicative value is something that accrues to the utterance itself. Instead of saying, as we may have seemed to do, that a certain configuration of contextual features 'results in' the speaker choosing a certain intonational treatment for his/her utterance, we will say, more correctly, that his/her intonation projects* a certain context of interaction. So

(28)   // the QUEEN of hearts //

can be said to 'project the assumption' that *hearts* is not selective. The assumption is part of the communicative value of the utterance, and we shall take it that this is the case even if there is nothing to justify it, either in the preceding text or in those areas of the shared biographies of the participants to which an analyst has access.

The fact that it is the speaker who decides what projection to make becomes very clear in the case of such a mismatch as:

(29)   Q: Which ace did you play?
         R: // the eight of HEARTS //

Failure to attend or hear properly here causes the respondent to project a context of interaction in which *eight* is existentially determined; the conflicting views of the situation will doubtless need to be resolved before the conversation can continue satisfactorily. Less obviously, the speaker's projection may incorporate features of a context of interaction to which he/she simply assumes the hearer will assent. We take it as a general linguistic principle that whenever a speaker has a choice of meaningfully different courses of action, he/she may exercise that choice to make his/her utterance mesh with some presumed state of affairs already existing; or he/she may exploit* his/her opportunity to choose, and represent the state of affairs in the light he/she wishes his/her hearer to see it in. If he/she chooses to do the latter, he/she must, of course, have regard to what the hearer will be likely to accept.

To illustrate exploitation of the prominence system, we will compare:

(30) Q: Did you say 'insolent officer'?
      R: // <u>NO</u> // insolent of <u>FIC</u>ial //

(31) Q: Who sent you away?
      R: // an insolent of <u>FIC</u>ial //

In (30) we can readily see that the respondent's projection is calculated to match the recently-created situation: there are evident grounds for treating *insolent* as non-selective. In (31) there are no such grounds. Unless there is something in the wider context, a possibility we should want to take into account if we were dealing with a specimen of real data, we have to interpret the response as projecting an understanding that, in the context of *officials*, the epithet is non-selective. To put it another way, the speaker sets up, for the purposes of the present conversation, a world in which there are no officials who are *not* insolent, and assumes that his/her hearer will see it this way too. The relationship between adjective and noun is similar to that in such common collocations as // an old <u>WITCH</u>// and // blushing <u>BRIDE</u>// , the intonation treatment of which usually assumes a world in which all witches are old and all brides blushing. In this aspect of its interpretation, (31) contrasts with

(32)   // an INsolent of <u>FIC</u>ial //

in which *insolent* is presented as a selection from a set of epithets in the existential paradigm, presumably because of its special appropriateness to this particular official.

It is because the distribution of prominence depends upon speakers' decisions, and because in making their decisions speakers are able to exploit the meaning potential of the system, that we cannot satisfactorily set up an explanation of the significance of prominence in terms of 'predictability'. At first sight, there seems to be good reason for offering such an explanation. In most of the examples we have used we could probably expect hearers to guess the non-prominent word even if, for some reason, they failed to hear it. When the context of interaction is such that it precludes selection, it would seem to be a natural corollary that anyone involved in the conversation would be able to fill the slot without difficulty. We have to keep in mind, however, that prominence is distributed by speakers, while guessing is a hearer's activity. Even if the former were constantly trying to fit his/her behaviour to the expectations of the latter, there could be no guarantee of perfect meshing all the time: as we have seen, situations would inevitably arise in which the true state of understanding between participants was not as it was judged to be. And to the extent that a speaker does not do this, but exploits the prominence system to project a context of interaction which suits his/her current conversational ends, the discrepancy between what is non-prominent and what can be guessed will be greater.

An extreme, but by no means untypical, case will help to reinforce the point just made. Consider the following as the opening of a conversation:

(33)   Q: Whatever's the matter?

       R: // the <u>BOSS</u> has been sacked //

It would not usually be the case that the first speaker would be able to predict *sacked*. Indeed, the implication of the response seems to be that being sacked is a highly unexpected thing to happen to the boss. If we compare the response with other possible versions, like

(34)   // the BOSS has been <u>SACKED</u> // or

(35)   // the <u>BOSS</u> // has been <u>SACKED</u> //

it becomes clear that the exclamatory force, the impression given of news coming out of the blue, is at least to some extent due to the non-prominent presentation of *sacked*. (We shall consider another possible contributory factor in Appendix A.) How, then, does this observation square with all we have said?

The explanation seems to be that, by deciding to present the word as non-selective, the speaker projects a world in which it *would* be non-selective, that is to say a world in which the question of who has been sacked has already been raised. We can invent a conversational setting which provides transparent motivation for the same response:

(36)   Q: But surely no-one has been sacked!

       R: // the <u>BOSS</u> has been sacked //

The response in (33) can be interpreted by saying that it is presented as if the discourse conditions were as they are in (36). An alternative conversational device, and one that we can invoke without making any special reference to intonation, helps to illuminate this particular use of projection. It is easy to imagine a conversation starting thus:

'Who do you think has resigned? The boss!'

If this occurred, there would be no necessary presumption that the person addressed had actually given any thought to the matter at all. Both this and (33) can be thought of as ways of producing a shock effect by beginning *in medias res*. The first introduces the question of who has resigned as if it were a burning one, so as to increase the impact of the disclosure. The second produces a rather similar effect by precipitating the hearer into a world in which the question is regarded as having already been asked.

The possibility of exploitation, particularly when it leads to the production of examples like (33), may seem to make difficult the attribution of a common significance to the prominent/non-prominent choice in the way we have proposed. If it has to be conceded that a speaker may project virtually any context of interaction, including some that have no kind of 'reality' outside his own private intentions, how can we claim that our general interpretation in terms of projected context is the proper one? The answer to this is the consideration that determined how we began this chapter. For any utterance, it is possible to invent a previous utterance which makes explicit whatever contextual implications the former projects, so that informants will recognise the appropriacy of the pair. Our examples (30) and (36), for instance, supply explicit contexts of interaction whereby the implicit projections of (31) and (33) can be tested. Conversely informants will recognise when we invent contextualising utterances that contradict the implications of the item we are interested in. The pair

(37)   Q: What's happened to the boss?
        R: // the <u>BOSS</u> has been sacked //

is heard as anomalous because (a) the question specifies *boss* and there-fore sets up a situation in which it is non-selective, and (b) it is assumed that more than one thing could have happened to the boss, so that *sacked* should be selective.

All intonation choices are available for exploitation, so it is worth reiterating and making general the argument for attributing a single communicative value to all instances of any particular choice, whether there are grounds for making a direct assessment of the context of interaction or not: the context that any utterance projects can be made explicit by inventing previous utterances which do, and which do not, make the expected contextual assumptions.

It is, of course, only because it is exploitable that the prominence system – or any of the other intonation choices for that matter – figure in an account of the communicative value of utterances. If the distribution of prominence were a necessary consequence of other choices that either speaker might make, or of any objectively observable view of what the discourse conditions were 'really' like, we should not be interested in it. Prominent syllables are not reflexes: we have to regard them as embodying speakers' choices from known alternatives.

Sense selection

We must now re-examine the notion we have designated selection. To do so, we will first consider the three examples following:

(38) || the QUEEN of hearts ||

(39) || an insolent of FICial ||

(40) || the BOSS has been sacked ||

It will be recalled that we said *insolent* was non-selective in (39) in that the speaker projected a world in which there were no officials who were *not* insolent. In stating the matter in this way, we were glossing over a difference between this example and (38) that we must now attend to. It happens that, in the case of the latter, all other words that we could entertain as possible fillers for the slot in question – *diamonds*, *spades* and *clubs* – must always have the existential value *not hearts*. Because of this, we were able to discuss selection in a very simple way as involving one word rather than others. If we compare (39) with this, it becomes evident that, in many situations, a very large number of epithets might be appropriate to replace insolent in the strict physical sense of filling its place between *an* and *official*. A plausible list might include:

	insolent	
a(n)	elderly	official
	temporary	
	etc.	

It is well within the bounds of possibility, moreover, that a particular official could be *insolent*, *elderly* and *temporary* at one and the same time. When we spoke of *insolent* as being presented as non-selective, there was clearly no intention of excluding all the words that might fill the slot. All that was excluded was any word whose value was incompatible with *insolent* (perhaps, for instance *kindly*, *attentive* or *obliging*). The existential paradigm we have to reckon with in such cases as this comprises not all possible physical replacements permitted by the context of interaction, but only those whose values are on the same sense dimension*, that is to say only those whose values are incompatible with each other.

We have taken it for granted that *insolent*, *elderly* and *temporary* are on different sense dimensions, so that no two of them would feature in the same existential paradigm. It is important to recognise, however, that this would not necessarily be true in every case. If there is an ongoing understanding that it is young officials who are insolent, or that insolence comes with the achievement of permanent status, non-prominent *insolent* might project a world in which the official was *not elderly* or *not temporary*. The context of interaction on which the efficiency of conversation depends includes a shared awareness of how words are existentially deployed with respect to each other on different sense dimensions. The assumed relationships are not necessarily those that are customarily thought to inhere in the abstract lexicon of the language.

Examination of (40) forces us to take a further step and abandon our working supposition that it is institutionalised 'words' that constitute the existential paradigm. We have said that in

(40)   // the BOSS has been sacked //

sacked is non-selective. Following our argument as we have developed it so far, we should have to say that the only words which could replace it without projecting an incompatible context of interaction would be words from the same sense dimension. There seems to be little doubt that essentially the same discourse conditions would have been projected if the speaker had said

(41)   // the BOSS has been fired //

and we can scarcely regard this change as amounting to a switch to a different sense dimension. Although the speaker signals the non-selective function of *sacked*, it is evident that there is an existential choice of some kind:

$$
\text{The boss has been} \begin{vmatrix} \text{sacked} \\ \text{fired} \end{vmatrix}
$$

This apparent counter-example to our general rule remains anomalous only so long as we retain our characterisation of the paradigm in terms of word selection. The same context of integration will be projected, whichever word is chosen, provided they both represent the same existential sense*.

The adjustment we need to make to our description, in order to accommodate (41) and many similar examples, is to regard the existential paradigm as comprising not a set of linguistic items ('word' or 'syllable') but as a set of mutually incompatible senses*. When, in a given context of interaction, we find that the choice between a pair of equally available words does not constitute a sense choice, we will say that a relationship of existential synonymy* holds between them.

It may well be that *sacked* and *fired* would be existential synonyms in virtually any context of interaction we might contrive for them. This is obviously related to the fact that, as uncontextualised dictionary items, they would normally be regarded as synonyms. The more common state of dependence on here-and-now considerations can easily be demonstrated, however, by considering the following as alternative utterances:

(42)   // the boss has been <u>SACKED</u> //

(43)   // robinson's been <u>SACKED</u> //

Clearly, *the boss* and *Robinson* are synonymous – which is to say that the two utterances project identical contexts of interaction – only in those situations where they are recognised as alternative labels for the same individual.

Returning now to example (38), we can see another reason why a phrase like *the queen of hearts* is suitable for introducing the notion of selection with the minimum of complication: for most practical purposes, there is a one-to-one relationship between the senses that are represented by *queen* and *hearts* and the words themselves. Even in saying this, however, we are overlooking the fact that at a particular stage in a particular game *hearts* may be *trumps*. Furthermore, habitual card-players and even adherents of a certain game, may have their own alternatives to the standard nomenclature: *Jacks* may be *knaves* and *twos, deuces*.

If two words can be used to represent the same existential sense, we must not, of course, assume that the choice between them is an insignif- icant one. One way of summarising much of this chapter is to say that matter presented non-prominently is intended to reify understandings already negotiated between speaker and hearer. The choice of *sacked* or *fired* may be seen as reifying understandings about the appropriacy of words in a situation where the identity of their senses is recognised. Like most informal vocabulary, such words are current in more-or-less restricted circles; by choosing one rather than the other the speaker projects an understanding that he/she and his/her hearer are members of that group – socially, geographically or historically defined – who use *this* word rather than the other. The point is demonstrated even more clearly if we compare either of the synonyms we have considered with another, more formal one:

(44)   // the <u>BOSS</u> has been dismissed //

In so far as a speaker who presents some part of his/her utterance as non- selective makes creative use of his/her ability to choose between existen- tial synonyms, he/she does so in order to make fine adjustments to the taken-for-granted background – to modulate from a world in which 'Jack of Hearts' is the preferred form to one in which 'Knave of Hearts' is current. Choices are understood to be made between modes of expression rather than between senses expressed.

Distribution of prominence in words

Before proceeding further, we must extend the scope of our description by abandoning the convenient, but strictly false, correspondence between 'prominent word' and 'prominent syllable'. We have so far assumed that each prominent syllable serves to give prominence to a word, and we have now seen that prominent words realise sense selections. It has been possible to get this far on the basis of such a simplifying assumption because of the empirical fact that when English words of more than one syllable are used in context, it is unusual for more than one of them to have selective function. Often, a non-promi- nent syllable is the only one available in the general paradigm. Thus, in

Are you com*ing*
It's hard*ly* worth it
I shoul*dn't* try

the rules of the language system ensure that there is no more opportunity for the speaker to select at the italicised syllable than there is in the
single-syllable words we considered in examples like:

The queen *of* hearts

Over and above the effects of the rule system of the language, the
understanding that characterises the context of interaction precludes
the possibility of there being alternatives in many other places, so that
for virtually all words there is existential choice at one syllable only. This
is the kind of assertion that could only be fully justified by examining a
large amount of data. We will do no more at this point than show how its
truth is borne out in an arbitrarily-chosen sample: we will examine all
the words having more than one syllable in the sentence that begins this
section.

> *Be* fore *pro* ceed *ing* furth *er* we must *ex* tend the scope of our
> *des* crip *tion* by *a* ban *don* ing the *con* ve *ni ent* but strict *ly* false
> *corr es* pon *dence be* tween prom *in ent* word and prom *in ent*
> syll *a ble*

If the words are examined in isolation, alternatives readily suggest
themselves for some of the syllables we have marked as non-selective:

					ex				*des*		*tion*
pro				*er*							
	ceed	ing,	furth			*in*	tend	,	crip		
suc				*est*					*pres*		*tive*
					con						

Some of these alternatives are eliminated by grammatical constraints:
we could not, for instance, have '. . . extend the scope of our descriptive
. . .'. The remainder are ruled out by contextual implications. Selection in
the appropriate general paradigms might produce the perfectly grammatical 'Before succeeding further we must extend the scope of our

prescription', but for anyone following the argument we are trying to develop, this is palpable nonsense. As usual, the existential paradigm, which depends upon the here-and-now state of understanding between the producer and recipient of the message, classifies more syllables as non-selective than the general paradigm would.

In performing an exercise like the one we have just completed, we are in danger of overlooking two facts. One is that the assertion we are making applies to the spoken realisation of the language: the question of how far the generalisation holds when spellings, not sounds, are taken into account is an entirely separate one, and one which we shall not confront. The other is that in any spoken version of our sentence we should not expect that there would necessarily be any prominent syllable at all in every polysyllabic word: some of the latter might be eligible for presentation as non-selective when considered as whole words. The treatment of the second *prominent* might, for instance, reflect the fact that in the context

(45)   // between PROMinent <u>WORD</u> // and prominent <u>SYL</u>lable //

there is no existential alternative. We have not, of course, said in this section that words do *not* occur with more than one prominent syllable: the citation form of words like // CON tro VER sial // and // U ni VER sity // is evidence to the contrary. Something will be said of the conditions under which such two-prominence forms are found in later chapters.

Syntagmatic organisation

The usefulness of the concept we have referred to as 'paradigm' as a heuristic device depends upon its being used in conjunction with the complementary concept, 'syntagm'. To state the matter very informally, selected language items – whether words or anything else – are not merely strung together in a chain; they contract relations with each other along the chain, or syntagmatic dimension, so that it is possible to identify internally-related entities of larger scope, and to regard these entities also as selections from a paradigm. An example from grammar will serve to amplify the point. If we examine the pair of sentences

John has left
John's new secretary left

we can quite properly say that each word in each sentence is a member
of the general paradigm associated with the slot it occupies: that is to say
we can think of each whole sentence in terms of the selection the
speaker makes at each word. Most people would agree, however, that this
way of looking at things fails to capture an important aspect of the
grammatical organisation of sentences, an aspect that is revealed in an
alternative representation of the selection:

| John | has left |
| John's new secretary | left |

Grammarians have used a variety of labels, like phrase, group and clause,
for the units that enter into the larger paradigms, sometimes postulating
a hierarchy or 'rank' scale, so that each syntagm is thought of as fitting
into another. The whole arrangement then provides as many different
kinds of syntagmatic selection as there are ranks in the hierarchy.

In order to show the relevance of the syntagm to our present interests,
we will return to the conversational fragment:

(22)   Q: What card did you play?
        R: // the QUEEN of HEARTS //

When discussing the response earlier, we said that *queen* and *hearts* were
selections from existential paradigms of thirteen and four members
respectively. An equally plausible claim would be that the tonic segment
considered as a whole constituted a selection from a single set of fifty-two
members. Instead of the diagram

	Queen		hearts
(the)	Ace	of	spades
	etc.		etc.

we might propose

	Queen of hearts
(the)	Ace of spades
	etc.

It happens that, for all practical purposes, both interpretations of this
particular example amount to very much the same thing. Another

invented example will show that this is not always the case and will suggest that, for some purposes at least, we must prefer the second way of representing selections:

(46)   Q: Who was your partner?

	Tom Smith
R: It was	Harry Brown
	etc.

It is unlikely that any real respondent would be able to count among potential partners people whose names consisted of all possible combinations of all their first and second names: knowing a Tom Smith and a Harry Brown does not mean also knowing a Tom Brown and a Harry Smith. A realistic view of possible responses – that is to say the set of options from which the respondent makes his/her selection – has to take into account combinatorial constraints as well as the factors that limit selection at each of the two places. Moreover, the set of possible responses might include:

	Tom Smith
(it was)	a friend of Mary's

We need not labour the point that, because the grammar of the two responses is not compatible, there is no possibility of making viable new responses by changing *Tom* to *friend* or *Smith* to *Mary's*. Finally, the respondent may have been selecting from

	Tom Smith
(it was)	the vicar
	etc.

that is to say, from a set which includes both extended tonic segments, as in // TOM SMITH // and minimal ones, as in // the VICar //. In these circumstances we cannot even begin to exchange items occupying a 'first' and 'second' slot. It is evident that, in order to take account of some aspects of the pattern of spoken discourse, we have to regard selection as involving the larger syntagm, that realised by the tonic segment, rather than the smaller one, the elementary carrier of a sense choice that we have associated loosely with the word.

Comparison with the methods of the grammarian is once again helpful. The latter's reason for recognising syntagms of different 'sizes' is that different grammatical options, like tense, number and mood, can be differentially associated with them: we may speak, for instance, of an imperative clause but of singular and plural groups. In a similar way, we must relate the different kinds of speaker choice to two different kinds of sense unit, the one realised by the word and the other realised by the tonic segment:

word	word	word	word
the	QUEEN	of	HEARTS

tonic segment

It is the smaller of these units whose value is affected by prominence, that is to say which is presented as either selective or non-selective. We have been able, in this chapter, to show on what basis speakers make decisions with regard to the prominence system simply by attending to words one at a time. In the following chapters, when we come to consider their decisions with regard to key, termination and tone, we shall see that the increment of meaning that derives from each of these choices attaches to the syntagm we refer to as the tonic segment. While it is proper to speak of prominence as an attribute of the word, each of the other three features is an attribute of the larger unit *considered as a whole*.

3

Key and termination

We have said that in tone units of both the minimal type

    // they're reQUIRED //

and the extended type

    // by adMINistrative PRACtice //

pitch-level choices serve to determine the key and termination of the whole tonic segment.

Any attempt to describe the communicative value of intonation has somehow to solve the problem of dealing with one thing at a time: of disentangling the effects of the three different choices associated with the tonic segment. For the purposes of this chapter, we shall discount temporarily the effect of the tone choice by assuming that this is always realised by a 'fall'. There remains the necessity for maintaining a conceptual separation between the effects of key and termination. If we begin with the minimal type of tonic segment, and entertain the possibility of there being three different presentations of the second tone unit in the following, discriminated by pitch level, we have to keep in mind that each realises two meaningful choices:

(47)   LOST // (high key and high termination)
    // he GAMbled // and LOST // (mid key and mid termination)
                  LOST // (low key and low termination)

It is more than likely, therefore, that the attempt we shall first make to characterise the significance of the key choice alone will leave the reader with a feeling that something important has been left unsaid.

High key

To account for the communicative value of the mid-key version in (47) we have to add nothing to what was said in the last chapter. *Lost*, being prominent, is presented as a selection from a set of possibilities defined by the context of interaction. We may surmise that, in a particular discourse setting, the existential paradigm projected would be something like:

$$
\text{He gambled and} \left| \begin{array}{l} \text{lost} \\ \text{won} \\ \text{broke even} \end{array} \right|
$$

To account for the high-key version, we have to take into account a new factor. *Lost* is still selective: the possibility is still acknowledged that, in the world of understanding the speaker attributes to the hearer, the man in question may have done other than lose. This much is implicit in the prominence. In addition, however, this version takes into account some kind of expectation that the gambler will *not* have lost: the situation projected is one in which he is expected to have done otherwise.

If we begin with the immediate, local effect of the high-key choice in *lost*, the easiest way to describe it is probably to say that it registers surprise. We could find many similar examples, too, to which the description could apply. We can take a step towards greater generality of statement if we think of this kind of expression of 'surprise' as comprising two interdependent, but conceptually separable, implications. First, the speaker assumes that, for present purposes, the relevant distinction is between *losing* and *winning*, any other alternative that the mid-key choice might admit being tacitly excluded from consideration. We shall say that, by associating high key with *lost*, the speaker projects a context of interaction in which the existential paradigm has two members. Secondly, we assume that the one he/she does *not* select is the expected one. And we shall say that a tonic segment thus presented has contrastive* implications.

We will explore the latter aspect – what we might think of as the negative implication of high key – first. To do this, we shall consider the case when it is associated with an item which is already, because of the nature of the language system, a selection from a set of two:

(48)　　|| it <u>WAS</u> john ||

Regarding *was* as the realisation of a polarity choice in this example, we can represent the general paradigm – and hence the existential paradigm also – exhaustively thus:

$$
\text{It} \quad \left| \begin{array}{c} \text{was} \\ \\ \text{wasn't} \end{array} \right| \quad \text{John}
$$

Even with mid key, therefore, *was* is a selection from two possibilities. What distinguishes it from a high-key version is the absence of any implied expectation that it would be otherwise. We could plausibly invent the context 'We always thought it might be John, and it was John'. With higher key,

(49)　　|| it <u>WAS</u> john ||

expressly contradicts a recent assertion, or a projected belief or assumption, that it wasn't:

> Speaker A:　What a pity it wasn't John.
> Speaker B:　It *was* John.

Of course, there is a sense in which positive polarity necessarily excludes negative polarity and *vice versa*; but this is the sense of the logician. What we are concerned with here is not the logic of the matter but the difference, in conversation, between *asserting that something was the case* (mid key) and *denying that it wasn't* (high key).

Before leaving this example, we will make two further observations. One has to do with the notion of 'surprise' which we made use of in introducing the discussion of high key. It is evident that (49) could occur in circumstances where it would be interpretable as an indication of surprise. Equally, though, the unexpected fact that it *was* John might occasion a wide range of reactions: pleasure, annoyance, alarm and many more. We might be tempted to abstract from all these and seek an attitudinal label which we could attach to some highest common factor; and certainly an element of surprise might be said to be an ingredient of many of them. One reason for not doing this, and preferring the greater generality of the formal description, is the difficulty of attributing the supposed emotional state: are we to say that the speaker registers his/her own surprise of his/her expectation that the hearer will be surprised? Questions like this take us outside the legitimate concerns of linguistic description. Our viewpoint is that the key system enables speakers to project an existentially valid contrast: to bring into sharp opposition a pair of possibilities and simultaneously exclude one of them. In doing this on a particular occasion, they may betray feelings, or anticipate feelings in their hearers, to which a more-or-less specific attitudinal label can be applied, but such specific interpretation depends on a multitude of factors. Once again, we must recognise the potential privateness of the relevant relationships: only the participants need know, for instance, whether some unexpected event is pleasing or annoying. Here, as elsewhere, we are interested in local interpretations only as a means to gaining access to the formal value of the intonation choice: that is to say the value that always accrues to it simply because of the fact that it *is* that choice.

The second observation also has to do with the important matter of speaker/hearer understanding. In order to avoid problems, we chose an example in which the polarity choice seems to be the one most likely to be associated with the contrastive implications of high key. We were thus able to speak with some plausibility of a binary opposition existing ready-made in the language system. It would not be impossible, however, for example (48) to be interpreted as projecting a tense selection, so that the existential paradigm would then coincide with a different general paradigm:

$$\text{It} \quad \begin{array}{|c|} \hline \text{was} \\ \\ \text{is} \\ \hline \end{array} \quad \begin{array}{|c|} \hline \text{John} \\ \hline \end{array}$$

A high-key version selecting *was* would then deny that it *is* John. The speaker's projection evidently includes the presumption that the hearer will hear *was* as a selection on the appropriate sense dimension. For a more complex example, which places even greater reliance upon the hearer's here-and-now ability to know what is being contrasted with what, consider

(50) $||$ he $\underline{\text{WILL}}$ go $||$

The paradigm projected by a mid-key version might here include, for instance

$$\text{He} \begin{array}{|c|} \hline \text{will} \\ \text{won't} \\ \text{may} \\ \text{would} \\ \text{etc.} \\ \hline \end{array} \text{go}$$

but that associated with the high-key version must be represented as

$$\text{He} \begin{array}{|c|} \hline \text{will} \\ \\ \text{x} \\ \hline \end{array} \text{go}$$

where the excluded member, x, may be assumed to be known only to the hearer.

Let us now consider the slightly different case where high key is associated with an open class item. In 'Look, it's John', the existential paradigm from which *John* is selected could well comprise a very large number of possibilities. In the version

(51) $||\underline{\text{LOOK}}\,||$ it's $\underline{\text{JOHN}}\,||$

we can think of *John* as a choice from among all those people, known both to speaker and hearer, whom 'it' might be. But, when the contrastive implications of high key are added, as in

(52) $||\underline{\text{LOOK}}\,||$ it's $\overline{\text{JOHN}}\,||$

the resulting '. . . it's John, not x' can be interpreted in either of two ways. The purport of the utterance might be 'it's not (as we might have expected) Peter' or it might be 'It's not any of the people whose appearance would have been more in line with expectations'. The latter alternative is frequently expressed as 'It's John, of all people!' The existential paradigms projected by the utterance might be either of:

		John				John
(i)	It's			(ii)	It's	
		Peter				x, y, z, etc.

We shall use the term particularise* for the special kind of contrast projected in (ii), where the existential opposition is between *one item* and *all other available items*.

On the basis of our examination of some minimal tonic segments, we can now make an interim summary and also clarify the terminology we need to proceed.

(i) We have referred earlier to what a speaker does when he chooses from an existential paradigm as *selecting*.

(ii) The special kind of selection which projects a binary opposition upon the existential paradigm and explicitly denies an alternative has been referred to as *contrasting*.

(iii) Those special instances of contrasting which reject the set of all existentially possible alternatives rather than rejecting one of a notionally symmetrical pair is referred to as *particularising*.

It is not difficult now to extend the account we have just given of the contrastive value of high key so that it takes in tone units having extended tonic segments. We saw in the last chapter that when a tonic segment has more than one prominent syllable it is best thought of, for some purposes, as entering *as a syntagm* into the speaker's selective procedures. We have only to show now that this applies when selection involves contrast. The following mid-key tone units resemble those in (47) and (51) in that each realises a sense selection from an existential paradigm which might, depending upon the context of interaction, have any number of members:

(53)   // he GAMbled // and LOST a FORtune //

(54)   // LOOK // it's JOHN'S new SECretary //

We can compare them with otherwise similar examples having high key in the second tone unit:

(55)   // he GAMbled // and ^{LOST a FORtune} //

(56) // LOOK // it's ^{JOHN'S} new SECretary //

In these, it is the whole of the tonic segment, '. . . lost a fortune' and '. . . John's new secretary' that is presented as one side of a binary opposition, excluding an implied alternative. It is, of course, a consequence of the way the tonic segment functions as a syntagm, regardless of whether there are two prominent syllables or one, that if we go on to verbalise the excluded member, it can take the form of either a minimal or an extended tonic segment:

(57)   // it's ^{JOHN'S} new SECRETARY // not JANE //

(58)   // it's ^{JOHN'S} new SECretary // not MARy ROBinson //

Particularising is exemplified in:

(59)   // it's ^{JOHN'S} new SECretary // of ALL PEO ple //

The only problem we encounter in introducing these examples at the present stage in our exposition is that our transcription conventions require us to specify a termination choice. In extended segments this is no longer determined by key. We have, in fact, assumed quite arbitrarily that high key is followed by high termination and mid key by mid termination. To avoid confusion, we must make clear that such correspondence is not automatic.

High and mid key with 'yes'

Special interest attaches to all intonation choices when they occur with the minimal utterances *Yes* and *No* and with the various items that serve as existential synonyms for them. We can prepare the ground for a number of later developments in our description if we focus here upon the effects of alternating high- and mid-key choices in this environment. We will consider first the common use of mid key in the second part of examples like:

(60)   Speaker A: I expect he's late.
        Speaker B: // YES // (= 'So do I')

(61)   Speaker A: I don't understand it.
        Speaker B: // <u>NO</u> // (= 'Neither do I')

On the basis of these examples we will postulate a sense value for mid-key *yes* (and *no*): it in some way associates the speaker with the *polarity* of the preceding speaker's utterance. The truth of this holds for these responses to yes/no questions:

(62)   Speaker A: Do you understand it?
        Speaker B: // <u>YES</u> // (= 'I do')

(63)   Speaker A: Don't you understand it?
        Speaker B: // <u>NO</u> // (= 'I don't')

It holds also for the third parts of:

(64)   Speaker A: Do you think it'll rain?
        Speaker B: I think so.
        Speaker A: // <u>YES</u> // (= 'So do I')

(65)   Speaker A: Is it going to rain?
        Speaker B: I don't think so.
        Speaker A: // <u>NO</u> // (= 'Neither do I')

There is one kind of apparent exception to this generalisation, but although it is common enough in conversation we need not dwell on it. It is exemplified by:

(66)   Speaker A: Isn't she a lovely girl!
        Speaker B: // <u>YES</u> // (= 'She is')

Negative interrogatives like this, whose polarity patently contradicts the understood state of affairs, are normally interpreted as though they had positive polarity. (Another one is 'Isn't it a miserable day!') We may interpret the response as something like 'Whatever you may *say*, I associate myself with what I know you *mean* – yes, she *is* lovely'.

Of more importance to our present argument are cases where there is real disagreement, involving opposition of sense as well as of grammatical form. As examples of such cases, consider:

(67)   Speaker A: I expect you're hungry.
        Speaker B: // <u>NO</u> // (= 'I'm not')

(68)   Speaker A: So you're not coming.

        Speaker B: // <u>YES</u> // (= 'I am')

Choice of high key for the contradictory *yes* or *no* follows from what we have already said: the first speaker indicates his/her expectation of one polarity choice and the second speaker selects the other.

If we tried to invent contradictory responses for some of the examples (62) to (66), using a high-key *yes* or *no* that went against the polarity expectations of the preceding utterance, we might consider that the result was unlikely to occur in polite conversation. Distinctly querulous overtones attach, for instance, to the response in:

(69)   Speaker A: Don't you understand it?

        Speaker B: // <u>YES</u> //

Contradiction has usually to be handled circumspectly if it is to avoid giving offence. Customary substitutes for high-key *yes*, like

(70)   // i <u>THINK</u> so //

and for high-key *no*, like

(71)   // ^{NOT} <u>REAL</u>ly //

help to reduce the friction. We shall see later (Chapter 5) that a choice of 'fall-rise' instead of a 'falling' tone can serve the same end. These refinements do nothing, however, to invalidate a generalisation we can now make: high-key *no* (or a synonym for it) has the communicative value *not yes*; high-key *yes* (or a synonym) has the value *not no*.

For our examples so far, we have chosen situations where we can assume a clear expectation in the context of interaction that either positive or negative polarity will be endorsed by the respondent: mid key is then chosen for the expected endorsement, while high key is chosen if the respondent reverses the polarity. We can take in further uses of *yes* with high key, and so increase the generality of our description by comparing these fragments of classroom discourse:

(72)   Teacher: What do you make the answer?
        Pupil: Eleven.
        Teacher: // <u>YES</u> //

(73)   Teacher: . . . and how many in a cricket team?
        Pupil: Eleven.
        Teacher: $|| \underline{\underline{\text{YES}}} ||$

We will assume that in the first of these the teacher is asking a
genuinely consultative question. He/She wants to compare the results of
his/her own computations with those of the pupil: his/her mid-key *yes*
has the value 'So do I'. In the second, it is fairly certain that the teacher
is asking the question to give the pupil the chance to show whether he/
she knows the answer and the need for evaluation customarily arises.
Classroom procedures will usually require that the teacher indicates
whether the pupil's response is the correct one or not. High-key *yes*,
which as we have seen discriminates explicitly against *no*, serves this
evaluating function. The paraphrase 'You are right, not wrong',
although seemingly tautologous if it is produced as a real utterance, can
be said to capture just what the teacher is telling the pupil. It is part of
the set of assumptions underlying this particular classroom game that
both possibilities are inherent in the situation until the teacher has
made his/her adjudication. Adjudication* involves the speaker in an
independent assignment of polarity; it thus differs from the act of
concurrence that mid-key *yes* realises. It is precisely by exercising this kind
of independence that respondents in the examples we examined earlier
declined to supply the expected *yes*, replacing it with a high-key *no*, and
vice versa.

The position we have now reached, of characterising a high-key *yes* (or
no) as adjudicating, and mid-key *yes* (or *no*) as concurring will provide us
with a starting point when we come to examine the communicative
value of termination later in the chapter.

Low key

Before doing so, we must first consider the third example in the set we
compared earlier:

(74) $||$ he $\underline{\text{GAM}}$bled $||$ and $_{\underline{\text{LOST}}} ||$

People who are asked to comment on the significance of the low-key
choice in *lost* usually do so to the effect that it sounds as though the

gambler's losing was a foregone conclusion: either the speaker's opinion of gambling or his/her assessment of the individual's luck is reflected in the implication that gambling and losing really amount, in this case, to the same thing. We shall take, as a first approximation, the idea that a tonic segment having low key is presented as being existentially equivalent* to the previous one. In order to take in extended tonic segments as well as minimal ones, we can make the same observation about:

(75) // he GAMbled // and LOST a FORtune //

Again, we find that it is the pitch-level choice at the first prominent syllable that affects the communicative value of the whole tonic segment, this time giving equative* value to *lost a fortune*.

We must now try to clarify the notion of existential equivalence. With mid key in *lost*, example (47) is heard as giving two separate pieces of information or – in our terms – as constituting two separate sense selections:

	gambled		lost
He	played safe	and	broke even
	etc.		etc.

Such a version projects a context of interaction in which all combinations of the two selections are possible. The world that provides the immediate setting for the utterance is one in which people gamble and win, play safe and lose, and so on. For comparison, we can represent the situation projected by the low-key version as

	gambled ·················· lost		
He		and	
	played safe		broke even
	etc.		etc.

where the broken line indicates an extra increment of value: it is not only that he gambled and lost; he did both in a world, existentially conceived, in which doing one necessarily entails doing the other. It is part of the speaker's meaning that the hearer should, for present purposes, assume a world in which such necessary entailment holds.

Note that this is not the same thing as projecting a world in which one of the linked elements is non-selective. This would be the result of saying:

(76) // he GAMbled and lost // or

(77) // he gambled and LOST //

Neither of these is easy to contextualise. Situations do not readily come to mind in which one might, for instance, produce these utterances in response to 'What did he do as well as lose?' or 'What did he do as well as gamble?' It is clearly a context of interaction in which one of these questions is assumed to have been raised that these versions project, and it is equally clearly a different one from that projected by the version that has *lost* as a low-key tonic segment. If we think informally of someone hearing either (76) or (77) being in receipt of *one* piece of information that he/she didn't have before – either that the person in question gambled or that he lost – then someone hearing the low-key version can be said to be in receipt of three pieces – that he gambled, that he lost, and that for present purposes the two are to be regarded as amounting to the same thing.

Another useful comparison can be made with

(78) // he GAMbled and LOST //

where *gambled* and *lost* are both presented as selective, but where the syntagm that coincides with the tonic segment is presented *as a whole* as a selection from a set of things he might have done, for instance:

	gambled and lost
He	refused to be tempted
	etc.

Presenting the two actions as if they were a single, unified choice from among the available possibilities does not imply that one is a necessary concomitant of the other. It is easy to imagine a speaker doing this in a situation where the significance of the two activities is that their effects are cumulative:

(79) // he GAMbled and DRANK // (. . . and ended in the bankruptcy court)

This presentation differs from

(80) || he GAMbled || and DRANK ||

only in that the two actions *are* yoked together as a single decision. The *and* in both (79) and (80) can be expanded to '. . . *and in addition* . . .'; that preceding the low-key choice expands rather to something like '. . . *and for present purposes this is to be taken as meaning that* . . .'.

We can distinguish two broadly different types of situation in which low key is used, depending on whether the speaker's intention seems to be to project an equivalence not necessarily yet known to the hearer, or to acknowledge a self-evident one. For an example of the first type, consider:

(81) || the SPEAKer was ILL || the _{LECture was CANcelled} ||

Here, both selections may be news to the hearer, as they would be if the second tone unit had mid key. The existential equivalence implied by low key would be likely to be interpreted as indicating a cause/effect relationship: the illness of the speaker had the predictable result that the lecture was cancelled. But notice that, because low key means nothing more than equivalence – in the present circumstances the two assertions amount to the same thing – the constituents can be reversed:

(82) || the LECture was CANcelled || the _{SPEAKer was ILL} ||

Now, the ordering of constituents coincides with effect/cause. In either version, the second tone unit may have had mid key, but the content of the two would not then have been presented as linked to the first, either as cause or effect. Where a simple additive relationship is intended, we shall expect mid key:

(83) || the LECture was CANcelled || i'd been WORKing all DAY ||
       my TOOTH was ACHing || (so I went home to bed)

For an example in which low key acknowledges an equivalence that is already self-evident, consider:

(84) || it is NOT the lawyer's JOB || to deCIDE what is RIGHT ||
       and _{WHAT is WRONG} ||

Deciding what is right, and deciding what is wrong, are patently two ways of describing the same activity, not two separate activities. In this utterance, which is adapted from a broadcast discussion, the speaker would probably be heard as spelling things out with condescending explicitness if he/she did not use low key. In the version we have transcribed, this effect is avoided: even while adding *what is wrong*, he/she acknowledges that it adds nothing to the value of his assertion. A similar and very frequent pattern is exemplified in:

(85)   // <u>YES</u> // i _{DO} //

A paraphrase of a concurring *yes* or *no* – *I can, it is, I am, indeed,* etc., depending on what the speaker is concurring with – has its tautological nature reflected in the low-key choice.

Something that the above observations do not explain, of course, is *why* speakers make such tautological additions. This is a matter we shall return to when we have considered the significance of termination choice.

Termination

To begin our investigation of the contribution that termination makes to the communicative value of an utterance, we must first recall the discussion on page 46 of the effect of key selection in the minimal utterance *yes*. We distinguished there between a high-key adjudicating function, which opposed *yes* to an existentially relevant *no* (= yes, you are right not wrong) and a mid-key concurring function which simply associated the speaker with the polarity choice of the previous utterance. Our next step is to recognise that when speakers are confronted by the need to select one of these versions of *yes* they may be influenced in their choice by the previous speaker's termination choice. By choosing high or mid termination, a speaker indicates an expectation that a responding *yes* will have a corresponding key.

Examples in which such expectations are realised are:

(86)   Speaker A: // DO you under<u>STAND</u> //
       Speaker B: // <u>YES</u> //

(87)   Speaker A: // DO you under<u>STAND</u> //

       Speaker B: // <u>YES</u> //

The import of A's utterance in the second of these, (87), can be made explicit thus: 'Tell me do you or do you not understand?' The high-key *yes* articulates Speaker B's assertion that he/she does: there is – he/she might be taken as asserting – no question of his/her not understanding. In (86) the first utterance is not so much a request for a decision as an invitation to confirm that the polarity of *do* is correct: the mid-key *do* articulates the expected concurrence (= Yes, I do).

    Speaker B may, of course, be unable to concur. If A has judged wrongly in assuming that he/she has understood, we shall expect something like:

(88)   Speaker A: // DO you under<u>STAND</u> //

       Speaker B: // <u>NO</u> //

Here, the high-key *no* contradicts the ongoing expectation that Speaker B will say *yes*. Notice that this example does more than illustrate once again the significance of key choice: it demonstrates also the way the constraints inherent in one speaker's termination choice may be overridden in what the next speaker actually does. It is convenient shorthand to speak of the expected termination/key correspondence as concord*, and an aid to conceptualisation to think of termination as a means whereby one speaker restricts another's freedom of choice. It is essential to keep in mind, however, that when two people are concerned there can be nothing like an absolute requirement to obey a 'concord rule'. The effect of termination can be described in the same way as we have described all other intonation choices: it decides an aspect of the context of interaction that the speaker projects. The latter will project an expectation that the hearer will adjudicate or concur, but there will inevitably be instances like (88) where the hearer's independent views of the situation will result in his/her not matching termination with key choice. We shall expect concord-breaking to occur at moments when there is a discrepancy between the ways the two parties assess the context of interaction.

    The way concord works can be illustrated rather clearly by examining the kind of grammatical tag we find, for instance, in:

I couldn't go, could I?

It is a well-recognised feature of tags of this sort that their constituents are fully determined by the first part of the structure they occur in. If we exclude 'I couldn't go, couldn't I?' as a different kind of item that requires different treatment, we can say that the verb *could*, its tense and polarity, and the choice of the pronoun *I* can all be predicted by simple rules, from what has gone before. It is impossible, moreover, to elaborate the tag by adding other constituents. In the terms we have used, this means that no such tag can represent a sense selection. Its contribution to the communicative value of the utterance can be only that which accrues to the intonation selections it realises.

We shall consider later the effect of tone choice in the tag, but will continue for the time being to assume that all tones are 'falls'. On this basis, we can compare:

(89) $//$ i $\underline{\text{COULD}}$n't go $//\underline{\text{COULD i}}$ $//$

(90) $//$ i $\underline{\text{COULD}}$n't go $//$ $\underline{\text{COULD}}$ i $//$

In (89) the assertion *I couldn't go* has mid key and thus meshes with a prevalent belief – perhaps made explicit earlier in the conversation – that there was no possibility of the speaker going. If the utterance had ended at this point, the concomitant mid termination would mean that any responding *yes* would be expected to be mid key – some kind of supporting *yes* that indicated the hearer's understanding that he/she *couldn't*. By adding the tag however, the speaker alters the utterance-final termination choice to high. The addressee is now invited to adjudicate: '. . . Could I, or could I not?' In (90), there is a high-key choice in the assertion and this gives it the force of a denial that the speaker *could* go. If he/she stopped at this point, the concord expectation would operate in such a way as to invite the hearer to say whether the denial was justified or not. The speaker evidently does not want his/her assertion to be evaluated in this way, since the mid termination in the tag invites concurrence.

A point to be noticed in passing is that in either of the examples we have just considered, a second speaker has a fairly easy way of avoiding the adjudicating or concurring stance he/she is invited to adopt. He/She may realise the expected key choice in a dummy item – one that is incapable of realising a sense selection – and then make an independent choice in the next tone unit. A possible rejoinder to (90) might be:

(91)   // WELL // <u>YES</u> // i think you <u>COULD</u> //

This satisfies the expectation of termination/key concord between speakers but refuses concurrence. There is little doubt that this purely formal accommodation to the first speaker's projection has a tempering effect upon the ensuing contradiction. Simultaneous concord-breaking and polarity reversal can be very abrasive.

The explanation we have so far offered in this section can be applied, as it stands, to only a tiny fraction of all the termination choices speakers make. For one thing, we have considered only those tone units that occur immediately before a change of speaker. We have assumed also that at such a point the new speaker responds with *yes*, *no* or some other item that can realise the alternative functions, either adjudicate or concur. It remains to be shown how the explanation can be generalised to apply to cases where either of these conditions is not satisfied.

We shall deal first with cases where there is a change of speaker, but no 'polar question' to elicit the *yes* or *no* response customarily associated with it. It seems, in fact, that there are probably no utterance types that could not be responded to with *yes* or *no*, given appropriate discourse conditions. We can begin to widen the interpretation we have proposed for high and mid termination by examining one of the less probable ones. *Wh-* questions are usually used to elicit non-polar information, but they do occasionally occur as the first element in pairs like:

(92)   Speaker A: // WHERE did he <u>FIND</u> it //
        Speaker B: // <u>YES</u> // (= 'I want to know that as well')

(93)   Speaker A: // WHERE did he <u>FIND</u> it //

        Speaker B: //<u>YES</u> // (= 'You are right – that is what we want to know')

In cases like these, there is no difficulty in applying the notions 'expectation of concurrence' and 'invitation to adjudicate' to the two versions of Speaker A's question. When we encounter *wh-* questions eliciting the kinds of response more commonly associated with them, however, we find these labels inappropriately precise:

(94) Speaker A: // WHERE did he <u>FIND</u> it //
      Speaker B: // in the <u>AT</u>tic //

(95) Speaker A: // WHERE did he ^{<u>FIND</u> it} //

      Speaker B: // in the ^{<u>AT</u>tic} //

In the first of these two, *attic* is simply selective: Speaker B states in which of the places it could possibly have occupied it was actually found. In the second, *attic* can be interpreted as particularising: it was found *there of all places*. Speaker B projects a binary opposition between this – pre-eminently unexpected – place, and all other, more likely ones. The effect of the termination choices in the two versions of A's question is to project an expectation that B will respond differentially in these two ways. In (94) A makes a straightforward request for information. In (95) his/her enquiry shows that an improbable answer is expected. It may be that the parties concerned have been jointly engaged in a search in all the likely places; whatever the precise situation may be, the communicative value of the question is something like 'Where on earth did you find it?'

For examples in which the same intonation choice has yet another local effect, compare:

(96) Speaker A: // he's SOLD his <u>CAR</u> //
      Speaker B: // <u>SOLD</u> it //

(97) Speaker A: // he's SOLD his ^{<u>CAR</u>} //

      Speaker B: // ^{<u>SOLD</u> it} //

Neither of our notional labels fits these exactly. In (96) it appears that the first speaker is providing factual information that the second does not yet possess. In these circumstances, the latter could scarcely 'concur' in the sense we have attached to the word. It is rather that he/she indicates that he/she has no difficulty in accommodating the information in his/her world view – the sale seemed imminent, or sensible, or otherwise no more than was to be expected. And by choosing mid termination, Speaker A loads the disclosure with the expectation that it will be received in this way. By choosing high termination in (97), A anticipates a contrastive response: high-key *sold* intimates that this was *not* what

Speaker B expected to hear. We could, perhaps, express the meaning increments due to the first speaker's termination choices as:

'This will not surprise you,' and

'This will surprise you.'

Notice that, because // SOLD it // is a minimal tonic segment, it automatically selects a termination corresponding to its key. In (97) the second speaker does not merely satisfy the expectation of a high-key response: he/she also sets up the expectation of a further high-key contribution from Speaker A. This would most characteristically be an adjudicating *yes*, assuring B that the surprising news was true (that it was not untrue as seemed probable). The concord requirements of the mid-key/termination response in (96) would anticipate a concurring *yes*, as would befit a situation in which both the speakers' world views and real-world reality seem to be fully matched.

One further example will serve to show the operation of termination/key concord in another way:

(98)   // PUT it DOWN //

This kind of peremptory instruction is most likely to be given, perhaps, by an adult to a child. It can be said to anticipate concurrence in a special sense. It expects a non-verbal reaction, which may or may not be accompanied by an acquiescent mid-key *yes*, signifying *I will*. We can regard mid termination as the normal choice with such utterances, since people making them do not usually see themselves as inviting the party to adjudicate in any way. There is an obvious inconsistency between trying to control someone else's actions and simultaneously giving his/her the opportunity to make a judgment about what you are doing. Oddly enough, though, if the child does not 'put it down' at the first time of telling, crossness or exasperation is often expressed by something like

(99)   // PUT it DOWN //

an utterance which *seems* to be putting the child in the position of having to choose between *yes* (I will) and *no* (I won't). Sometimes, the invitation to decide is made even more explicit:

(100)   // WILL you put it DOWN //

(101)　　// PUT it $\underline{DOWN}$ will you //

Something that is very certain is that the adult does not expect the
invitation in any of these forms to be taken at its face value. It is rather
that, by seeming to issue it, the adult dares the recalcitrant child to say
no. The well-understood convention is that, since the anticipated high-
key *yes* or *no* would be quite inappropriate, there should be no verbal
response but prompt non-verbal activity.

The problem presented, with greater or lesser acuteness, by all these
examples is the one that will keep cropping up throughout this book. It
is the problem of giving some sort of notional characterisation to a
formal linguistic opposition. By starting with examples of a particular
kind we were able to see the distinction in terms of 'an invitation to
adjudicate' versus 'an expectation of concurrence'. Such glosses were
found, however, to reflect too precisely the particular contexts we had to
invent for our examples to be generally applicable. We cannot assume
that a fully general characterisation could be captured in a paraphrase at
all, but in so far as this is possible, it seems best to think of a choice
between active verbal intervention and passive acceptance on the hearer's part. The adjudication invited by many instances of high termination
is then conceived of as independent 'activity'; the concurrence expected
by mid termination is a manifestation of 'passivity'. To decide is to be
'active'; to go along with another's assessment of the situation is
'passive'. The formal statement avoids such conceptual problems: a
speaker's choice of high or mid termination projects an expectation of
continuance in high or mid key respectively.

When we speak of continuance in the last paragraph, we have in mind
continuance by another speaker. We have already recognised the need to
take account in our description of termination choices that occur in mid-
utterance. We can do this fairly simply by an extension of what has been
said so far. We will take it that in the following example there is no
opportunity for the addressee to intervene as new speaker after *ashamed
of himself*:

(102)　　// he OUGHT to be a$\underline{SHAMED}$ of himself // and i'm GOing to
　　　　 $\underline{TELL}$ him so //

There are, of course, many kinds of overt reaction the addressee may
evince, short of actually assuming speaker role. Anyone listening to an

extended monologue that is addressed to that person – as distinct from one that is merely overheard – is aware that even as hearer he/she has an important participating role. The supportive behaviour he/she feels called upon to provide may range from a murmured *yes*, through non-verbal noises like *mm*, to headnods and other non-vocal activity. Anyone who speaks in public will testify to the importance of this kind of feedback to the speaker's peace of mind. Whatever form it takes, each supportive event can be interpreted as an active or a passive response, and we can interpret the speaker's termination choices as projecting an expectation of a response of one kind or the other at certain points in the monologue. If the response is supportive and realised vocally, we can expect it to obey the same pitch-concord rule as we have seen operating between discrete utterances. If it is not vocalised, it seems likely that the two kinds of response will be indistinguishable; we need not entertain here the possibility of there being concurring and adjudicating head-nods that are systematically differentiated.

Our present concern is primarily with the contribution the termination choice makes to the communicative value of its containing utter-ance, and we can describe this with reference to example (102). Again we have to resort to paraphrase which will at best be clumsy and approx-imate. The first tone unit has some such force as 'Consider whether he ought or ought not to be ashamed of himself': the listener is asked to adjudicate. The second 'I'm going to tell him so' takes concurrence – in this case approval of the speaker's declared intention – for granted. The rhetorical device of seeming to give one's hearer an opportunity to judge and proceeding immediately to assume a consensus is well understood by orators, from market-stall cheap-jacks to aspirants to high political office. For a famous example, we can take:

> But Brutus says he was ambitious;
> And Brutus is an honourable man.   (*Julius Caesar* Act 3, Scene ii)

It is, of course, the actor who decides the intonation treatment of a dramatic text, but one reading which would seem to be justified is:

(103)   // but BRUTus // says he was am^BITious //
        // and BRUTus is an honourable MAN //

Here the high termination invites active consideration of the proposition that Caesar was ambitious, but by selecting mid termination for the following tone unit, the speaker projects an assumption that his audience will accept the description of Brutus as an honourable man without question.

It is not part of our argument that hearers necessarily provide overt reactions at each and every point where they would seem to be called for. At the risk of seeming to labour the point we will stress that expectation of a particular response is part of the meaning of the utterance, and this is all we are concerned with. Careful monitoring of one's own mute reactions to speakers goes a long way to confirm that listening sometimes demands acquiescence in what is said and sometimes involves exercising independent judgment. Unfortunately, this can scarcely be used as evidence. Our assertion that the distinction applies to cases where there is no overt reaction from a hearer, or where a reaction is apparently ambivalent (as, for instance, a nod of the head), depends upon extrapolation from cases where there is an audible and unambiguous response.

Simultaneous selection of key and termination

We have now associated different meaning systems with the two variables, key and termination. Even in doing so, we have had to acknowledge, however, that in minimal tonic segments there is no possibility of making the two selections independently. At first sight, this seems like a severe restriction upon the speaker's freedom of action. A speaker who has reason to select, say, high termination in

(104)   // is THAT $\underline{\text{TRUE}}$ //

can do so while still preserving a situationally appropriate mid key; but to achieve a similar termination choice in

(105)   // $\underline{\text{REAL}}$ly //

one unavoidably tags *really* with a meaning increment derived from high key. What we now have to consider is how it is possible for a speaker to achieve a desired termination choice in a minimal tonic segment without being committed to a choice of key which would not be valid in the intended context of interaction. To put the matter slightly differently, we shall be asking how a system which appears at first sight to place very tight constraints upon a speaker can actually allow in its operation for the measure of freedom that is evidently necessary.

We shall begin by examining more closely the relationship between different key choices. One possible source of flexibility might be the option the speaker has to make a particular key selection even if it does not strictly reflect his/her communicative intentions, simply to achieve a desired termination. To investigate this, we need to consider the conditions of compatibility between adjacent terms in the key system. We have said that the difference between the key choice and the termination choice in a particular tonic segment is never more than one 'level' in the three-term system. We shall assume, therefore, that when both choices are compressed into a single prominent syllable, the termination choice will not be more than one step above or one step below what we will refer to as the 'situationally appropriate' key choice. Considering only high and mid possibilities for the moment, there will be these situations:

high		actual key and termination
mid	'appropriate' key	

high	'appropriate' key	
mid		actual key and termination

In what circumstances can the 'actual' key choice (which is dictated by the need for a given termination choice) be substituted for a different 'appropriate' one without the result being a situationally invalid utterance? Are there contexts of interaction in which high key would be a conceivable choice while mid key was not, and vice versa?

The processes of simple selection that we have associated with mid key and of particularisation that we have associated with high key can be compared as follows:

(i) // the queen of <u>HEARTS</u> // : the queen of

> hearts
> diamonds
> spades,
> clubs

(ii) // the queen of ^{HEARTS} // : the queen of

> hearts
> (diamonds, spades,
> clubs)

From this we can see that any communicative purpose which is served by (i) is likely to be served by (ii). The effect of both is to present *hearts* as a selection from among all four suits. The fact that in (ii) the four are presented as being organised into a contrastive set of two will not usually prevent its being used where (i) would be adequate: on many occasions, an unmotivated choice of high key attaches particularising implications redundantly to the value of the tone unit. If we consider the negative implications of (ii), we find that these also are often redundant but tolerable in situations that are satisfied by (i). A speaker can often substitute 'X, not – as might seem to be the case – Y' for 'X selected from the set X and others' without noticeable effect on the context of interaction. A comparison with the relationship holding between lexical items might be helpful here. *Dog* and *spaniel* are said to be 'hyponymous', a statement we will relate informally to the fact that all spaniels are dogs but not all dogs are spaniels. We will say that *spaniel* carries more 'information' than *dog*. In general, if someone calls his/her dog a spaniel he/she may be providing information over and above what the situation demands, but little harm will be done. If, on the other hand, he/she calls it a *dog* when there is present need to specify *spaniel* essential information is lost. Similarly, if a speaker says

(106) // he's $\underline{\text{LOST}}$ //

in order to invite adjudication, he/she may attach unnecessary, but harmless contrastive implications to *lost* by reason of the concomitant high-key choice. If he/she seeks concurrence, with

(107) // he's $\underline{\text{LOST}}$ //

he/she cannot fulfil an intention he/she may well wish to fulfil of contradicting an ongoing belief that *he did not lose*.

It would be easy to imagine special circumstances in which the comments we made about *dog* and *spaniel* would be untrue. In the same way, we must stop short of suggesting anything like a hard and fast rule determining how high and mid key can be interchanged. It seems true, however, that a gratuitous step up in key to achieve high termination is more frequently tolerable than a gratuitous step down to achieve mid termination.

Consider now the relationship between mid and low key as it is illustrated in the pair:

(108) // he GAMbled // and LOST //

(109) // he GAMbled // and ₗₒₛₜ //

We can recognise a relation of hyponymy here if we notice that for (109) to be appropriate in any set of circumstances, (108) would have to be appropriate also; but (108) would not be appropriate in all situations where (109) was appropriate. (108) asserts that both events occurred; (109) asserts this and *also* that the two formulations are existentially equivalent. In this case it is the 'lower' choice that carries information additional to that carried by the 'higher' one. At first sight, then, the situation seems to mirror that which we discovered when comparing high and mid key. By gratuitously stepping up, the speaker stands to lose intended equative implications; by gratuitously stepping down he/she realises his/her intentions and projects other information besides. The favoured directionality for movement, that is to say that which sacrifices none of the communicative value of the utterance, would seem to be as summarised below:

high
↑
mid
↓
low

There is, however, a special constraint inherent in the equative function. The equative value of low key is not potentially redundant in the way we have said the contrastive value of high key often is. The 'additional information' it projects has to have some kind of justification in the context of interaction. Specifically, (109) can be appropriate in just those circumstances where it is appropriate to project an existential equivalence between gambling and losing. The low-key version would not be available if the events reported were related only in that they occurred in sequence:

(110) // he WASHED // and put a RECord on //

Our diagram therefore exaggerates the speaker's freedom to manoeuvre as between the mid and low choices.

Simultaneous selection

To pursue further the question of the flexibility of the system, we will reconsider the notion of selection that was discussed in the last chapter. We presented that discussion solely in terms of sense selection. So,

(111) // the QUEEN of HEARTS //

was said to have prominent *queen* and prominent *hearts* in order to project a context in which neither of these words realised an already-established sense. We have now seen that, in addition, they carry the phonological choices that determine the key and termination of the tonic segment respectively. This situation – the location of two choices made simultaneously at the same point in the left-to-right chain – can be represented as follows:

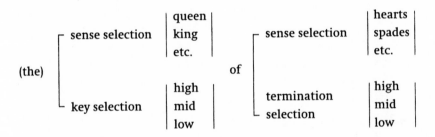

The next step is to appreciate that, since an intonation choice can be associated with a syllable only if it is prominent, the need to make a particular intonation choice may be sufficient reason for assigning prominence to a syllable. Even if it is no part of a speaker's intention to present *queen* as a sense selection, it may still be made prominent in order to achieve a desired choice of key or termination. If it is self-evidently not a sense selection – as for instance in a response to 'Which queen did you play?' – we can represent the situation as follows:

(the) ⎡ sense | queen |

       ⎣ key selection | high | (of hearts)
                          | mid |
                          | low |

The expedient of making a syllable prominent in order to carry an intonation choice serves a number of communicative purposes, some of which will be taken up in later chapters. For the moment we will note that it makes it possible for a speaker to make dissimilar choices of key and termination in a tonic segment when there would otherwise be no possibility of doing so.

4

Tone: proclaiming and referring

We saw in Chapter 1 that attending to the pitch movement that begins at every tonic syllable provides us with a working phonetic characterisation of five tones, the 'fall', the 'rise', the 'fall-rise', the 'rise-fall' and the 'level' tone. These constitute a five-way choice confronting the speaker at each tone unit he/she utters. In principle, he/she may choose any one of them; in reality, certain combinations of tone choice and lexical and grammatical features are more probable than others. If he/she does not choose one of the five, the tone unit will sound incomplete. We have now to investigate the communicative significance of the choices he/she makes.

A feature of the present description is that it associates a particular communicative value with each of the tones in a way that holds true for all occurrences of that tone. Very often it has been either stated or assumed that the significance of a choice depends in some absolute way on other factors in the environment. Thus a 'rise' may be thought to require one explanation when it occurs in a 'list' and quite another when it occurs in a 'question'. The position adopted here is that all such differences in local interpretation are to be traced to differences in the context of interaction: the meaning increment that any one of the five tones contributes is the same, regardless of its environment. To achieve this generality of statement, we are forced to gloss the value of the increment in somewhat abstract terms. In searching for ways to make the abstract meanings graspable, we have to keep in mind, moreover, that our concern is not finally with establishing a relationship between a particular tone and anything that might be said about what the non-linguistic world is like. As we have said earlier (see Preface) we are concerned to establish what relationships hold among parts of the language system. Our initial question is not: 'What is the communicative value of tone x?'; we have to ask rather 'What are the consequences of choosing tone x *in preference to another?*'

It turns out that the most illuminating account of tone is one which recognises among the five possibilities a number of sub-systems. It would be quite possible to treat all the tones as being simultaneously available choices at any point and then try to elucidate their respective values on the basis of simple mutual definition. We might propose an analogy with the way the lexical organisation of English deals with some fairly well-defined semantic field like the colours of the spectrum: any one term, say *red*, is then definable as denoting that colour which is *not* covered by all the other terms put together. Then, for instance, the value of the 'falling' tone would be regarded as covering that part of the area of the meaning system that is released by tone and not covered by the other four. It proves more satisfactory, however, to proceed by identifying separate binary oppositions within the total set. There is, of course, no way of justifying this approach in advance; justification would involve us in anticipating everything that will be said in this and subsequent chapters about the total pattern of meaning potential associated with tone. For the moment the procedure has to be taken on trust.

The P/R opposition

A pair of examples will serve as a starting point for investigating the opposition that is realised by the two tones most frequently found in many kinds of discourse, the 'fall' and the 'fall-rise':

(112) || \/ MARy <u>BROWN</u> || \ is a <u>TEACH</u>er ||

(113) || \ MARy <u>BROWN</u> || \/ is a <u>TEACH</u>er ||

Since these two utterances are identical in all other respects, we can attribute whatever differences there are between their communicative values to the differential distribution of the two tones we are presently interested in. One way of capturing the difference is to paraphrase the two examples thus:

> 'Talking of Mary Brown, she's a teacher.'
> 'Talking of teachers, Mary Brown's one.'

Very informally, we may say that the constituent that has a 'fall-rise' is already in play, conversationally: it is *what we are talking about*. The constituent that has the 'fall' is something freshly introduced into the conversation. The following pair are different grammatically, but similarly distinctive values attach to the two tone units in each:

(114) || ⋁̸ WHEN i've finished MIDdlemarch || ⭨ i shall READ
adam BEDE ||

(115) || ⭨ WHEN i've finished MIDdlemarch || ⋁̸ i shall READ
adam BEDE ||

Whatever the additional implications these two may have, we may be sure that (114) is spoken in circumstances where the hearer is expected to know – perhaps as a result of something said in the present conversation – that the speaker is in the process of reading *Middlemarch*; the intention of reading *Adam Bede* is declared as if it were an item of news. By contrast (115) addresses itself to the question, presumed to have been already raised in some way, as to when the speaker will read *Adam Bede*; what is presented as news is the intention of doing so after finishing *Middlemarch*. It is worth noting, in passing, that these interpretations still apply if the order of the grammatical constituents is reversed:

(116) || ⋁̸ i shall READ adam BEDE || ⭨ when i've finished
MIDdlemarch ||

(117) || ⭨ i shall READ adam BEDE || ⋁̸ when i've finished
MIDdlemarch ||

In these two examples, as in the preceding four, it is the tone unit having the 'fall-rise' that contains what has been raised already, that with a 'fall' that contains the news. We shall speak of the former as a referring* tone and the latter as a proclaiming* tone.

By replacing the graphic symbols ⋁̸ and ⭨ by the letters *r* and *p*, as in

(114) || *r* WHEN i've finished MIDdlemarch || *p* i shall READ adam
BEDE ||

we can avoid an over-precise suggestion of the phonetic realisation of the tones and foreground instead the abstract, formal opposition in the language system to which we shall give the term P/R opposition*: as we said in Chapter 1 we must always leave room in our conceptual framework for the possibility that the phonetic shape of any tone will vary from speaker to speaker and perhaps, within a given speaker's usage, between one occurrence of that tone and the next. In practice, there are few problems in applying the traditional phonetic criteria, but our real concern has to be with *what counts as* an r tone and *what counts as* a p tone in the linguistic expectations that speaker and hearer share.

The abstract nature of the P/R opposition has to be kept in mind also when we try to conceptualise the communicative consequences of selecting one term or the other. The rest of this chapter will be devoted to elaborating, and trying to make as precise as possible, the significance of the speaker options to which we have given the suggestive labels 'referring' and 'proclaiming'. How can we grasp, in terms that have general application, the difference between what the speaker does when referring and what the speaker does when proclaiming?

Speaker-hearer convergence

We can take one step towards answering the question if we represent a central feature of every verbal encounter diagrammatically:

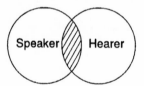

The intersecting circles represent the world views of speaker and hearer respectively at the moment of utterance of a tone unit. We can speak of the shaded area as the 'common ground' they share, and then proceed to consider in what ways the metaphor can be appropriately interpreted for our needs.

In each of the six examples we have used in this chapter, the matter of the tone unit having referring tone is presented by the speaker as being already present in the common ground. To revive another metaphor we have used, it is already 'in play' in the conversation. When the speaker associates a stretch of his discourse with referring tone, he/she indicates that this part of the discourse will in no way alter the state of speaker/hearer convergence that our diagram encapsulates. The matter of the tone unit having a proclaiming tone is presented as not yet present in the common ground. By proclaiming some part of his/her discourse, the speaker declares his/her expectation that this will increase the area of convergence: a very rough approximation, which applies well enough to our six examples, but which proves too simple when we come to examine the significance of the P/R opposition in the language at large, would be that this is the part that tells the hearer something he/she didn't already know.

The state of convergence is, of course, an aspect of that larger postulate, the context of interaction, to which all intonation choices are related. We have already seen that the context of interaction is to some extent a product of the ongoing conversation: to the extent that this is the case, referring tone units can be seen to make retrospective reference to elements in the recorded text. But what a speaker may legitimately regard as being in play is not limited to what has been previously mentioned. When a newsreader begins a fresh item in his/her bulletin

(118) // r in the MEN's SINGles final // r at WIMBledon // . . .

he/she assumes that listeners will be expecting a reference to this event on this particular Sunday in July and that they will also know where it takes place. This is the device whereby he/she relates to a taken-for-granted focus of interest before telling hearers what they are assumed not to know – who won. Similarly, a lecturer may open his lecture

(119) // r the LATer novels of DICKens // . . .

on the strength of a presumption that, by public notice or some other means, the audience have already been appraised of what the lecture is going to be about. In exchanges like

(120) Speaker A: // p WHENdo they CLOSE //
       Speaker B: // p FOURo'CLOCK // r at THIS time of year //

the respondent will be heard as articulating the implication treated by Speaker A as already-negotiated common ground – that the latter wants to know when they close *now*.

The addition of *at this time of year* in (120) does little more than spell out the self-evident: in any real conversation it would be fairly certain that Speaker A wasn't enquiring about closing time at any other season. In such circumstances, and in conversational openers like

(121) // r i've COME to SEE you // (to ask you about . . .)

proclaiming tone would sound very odd. What is physically apparent to the hearer will not usually be stated unless its status as part of the shared world is acknowledged by choice of referring tone. The fact that we can point to certain highly predictable tone choices like these must not, however, be allowed to obscure the fact that decisions concerning tone are, like all other decisions in the system, made by speakers; and, as we have said before, wherever there is a requirement to decide, there is an opportunity to exploit. A parenthetical

(122) . . . // r AS we all <u>KNOW</u> // . . .

projects a state of convergence which may have little or no foundation in reality. A less palpable instance of exploitation is:

(123) . . . // r we HAVE to re<u>MEM</u>ber // <u>THAT</u> // r they're re<u>QUIRED</u> //
        (to take these decisions on paper)
(See page 6 for the context.)

Here, the need to keep in mind certain facts about the decision-making procedure is introduced as if it had already been negotiated: other participants in the discussion need not in reality have accepted that these facts are important at all, and the speaker may be very well aware that they haven't. The reference to *requirement* may also be contentious, but by insinuating common understanding that the officials have no choice as to procedures, the speaker gives his/her judgment the status of agreed background against which his/her subsequent assertions are to be heard.

Another way of conceptualising the significance of the P/R opposition, which actually does no more than extend the applicability of the 'common ground' metaphor we have been developing, is as follows. Seen from one point of view, verbal communication is a linear and cumulative process which has as its intended outcome an increase in the area of speaker/hearer convergence. Some stretches of discourse constitute a step forward in this process, while others do not. The significance of the proclaiming tone is that, by producing it, the speaker offers to further the process by changing the hearer's world view; the referring tone units can be characterised negatively as ones in which the speaker recognises that he/she is saying nothing that will constitute a step forward. There are strings of tone units in which the alternation of consolidatory and world-changing matter can be recognised easily. Consider the answer in the following pair:

(124)   Speaker A: What will you do on your day off?
Speaker B: // r WHEN i've prepared my LECture // r if there's any TIME left // p i shall GO into TOWN // r and AFter THAT // p it will dePEND on the WEATHer // p perHAPS i shall play TENnis // r if it's FINE // r and if there's anyone aROUND // r OTHerwise // p i'll WRITE some LETters //

Here, Speaker A asks B to 'tell' something – in our terms, to say something that will change A's world view. The first tone unit of the response tells nothing A does not already know: the fact that there is a lecture to be prepared is introduced as something already understood, and when it has been referred to, the two participants are in exactly the same state of convergence as A assumes they were in before. We can represent the tone unit graphically as a loop – an excursion into the common ground – which ends where it began:

When I've . . . lecture

The same is true of the second tone unit. B's dependence on having sufficient time to do anything else is also presented as something that will be understood, and constitutes another non-progressive loop:

When ...   if ...
lecture   left

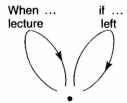

The third tone unit is presented as world-changing for A: it is a part answer to the enquiry, and constitutes a movement towards greater convergence – a step forward in the information-exchanging process that A has initiated:

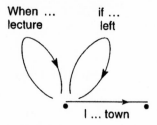

The whole utterance can now be seen as 'loops' which represent shared understanding that the speaker takes for granted, and increments which add up to what the listener is 'told':

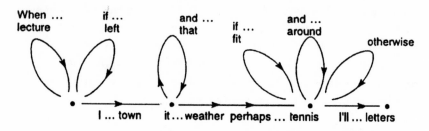

In this particular case, it is the background of self-evidently necessary conditions, and the temporal framework – the fact that the proposed activities have an order of priority – that make up the taken-for-granted portion of the reply.

We have said that Speaker A's question sets up an expectation that B will eventually say something that is world-changing, even if it is delayed by the intervention of a number of referring tone units. In this connection it is interesting to note the effect of tone choice in minimal responses. Consider:

(125)   Speaker A: // p WHERE does he COME from //
        Speaker B: (i) // p SOMEwhere in SCOTland //
                   (ii) // r SOMEwhere in SCOTland //

With a proclaiming tone, the response fulfils the common expectation associated with an enquiry. B says something that furthers ongoing business: it tells A what A wants to know. With a referring tone, B can be heard as declining to take the step he/she is asked to take. The response is then presented as an excursion into assumed common ground rather than as a step towards the greater convergence that A evidently desires.

The most likely interpretation of B's behaviour would seem to be that A is understood to want information of a more precise nature than the former can provide – the question might, perhaps, be understood to mean '. . . from Aberdeen or Glasgow?' The answer to *this* question is 'I don't know', but instead of saying so in so many words B makes a tone choice which makes clear that this is not the kind of information A really wants: 'Instead of taking matters further in the way I know you want me to, I can only reiterate what I assume you already know'. When referring tone units are said to imply a 'but . . .' it is usually because the discourse conditions are such that the speaker is expected to provide information or give an opinion but chooses instead to confirm related – and perhaps more acceptable – understanding:

(126)   Speaker A: He's a good player, isn't he?
       Speaker B: || r he TRIES hard ||

Speaker B endorses *this much* as common ground, but in so doing seems to imply an unwillingness to voice the proclaimed agreement that A evidently wishes to elicit. And in such a situation, what one declines to say may be of greater importance than what one says.

Reference and non-selection compared

Further insight can be gained into the significance of the P/R opposition if we compare the effect of choosing referring tone with the effect of assigning no prominence to the same element. At first sight, the projections made by these two speaker-decisions seem to have a great deal in common. We have, for instance, said that a tonic segment having referring tone is often presented as making backward reference to something in the text; and when we said earlier that *queen* was non-prominent in || the queen of HEARTS || we said that its non-selective status might be justified on the grounds that it had been anticipated in a preceding utterance, such as 'Which queen did you play?' In so far as they both can represent something as what we might loosely call 'given' in the context of interaction, the two decisions appear to have a similar effect upon what is projected. We can further clarify the significance of both, and at the same time further refine the way we conceptualise the communicative value of the P/R system, by exploring the difference.

The two can be brought into clear contrast in:

(127)   Q: Is there anyone in the office?
R1: // p i THINK jill's gone HOME //
R2: // p i THINK // r JILL'S // p gone HOME //

Response 1 amounts to very much the same thing as 'I don't think there is'. By making *Jill* non-prominent, the speaker projects a context of interaction in which there are no alternatives: in which *anyone* can only be *Jill*. Only an element of friendliness or warmth toward Jill separates this response from // p i THINK she's gone HOME //. In response 2, however, the fact that Jill has gone home does not necessarily mean that the office is empty. *Anyone* is interpreted as 'any member of the set of people who might be in the office', and the tonic segment with referring tone answers selectively with respect to it: 'Jill has gone, but I don't know about anyone else'.

We can show that non-prominence is unlikely to be a credible alternative to referring tone in circumstances where selection is probably involved. The lecturer to whom we attributed the opening

(128)   // r the LATer novels of DICKens // ...

would probably not have been able to begin

(129)   // p the later novels of dickens have a SPECial INTerest //

because to have done so would have been to project an assumption that the topic of his/her opening paragraph was predetermined precisely. The truth of the matter would almost certainly be that within the area of understanding one could reasonably expect to take for granted in such a situation there would be a number of different candidates for opening topic. An advertised title which prepared the audience for (128) might equally well prepare them for:

(130)   // r MUCH victorian FICtion // ...   or

(131)   // r BLEAK HOUSE // ...

While the sense of the tonic segment in (128) can present matter that is assumed to be present in the common ground and therefore to qualify for choice of referring tone, it evidently represents a sense selection in that it singles out one of the possibilities that are assumed to be existentially available.

At the other extreme, there are cases where we can point to the comparative unlikelihood of a non-prominent element being presented prominently with a referring tone:

(132)   Q: Which queen did you play?
      R1: // p the queen of HEARTS //
      R2: // r the QUEEN // p of HEARTS //

Response 2 seems far less likely than response 1 because *queen* is manifestly not selective. It is interesting to note, however, that if the second version did occur, the speaker would be heard as responding as if there were a choice; it would project a context of interaction in which the denomination of the card was still not determined, even though it had just been mentioned. There would be some suggestion that the first speaker might have made a mistake, or that the respondent had possibly misheard, so that re-selection was necessary in the response.

The social significance of tone choice

Slightly more complex issues are raised by examples like:

(133)   // p i DON'T actually LIKE it //

(134)   // p but frankly i DON'T want to GO //

When adverbials like *actually* and *frankly* are interpolated into certain kinds of conversation, their strong tendency to occur without prominence accords with the fact that they seldom constitute selections in a sense paradigm. If our imaginary speakers had simply said 'I don't like it' or 'I don't want to go', the precision of the first assertion and the sincerity of the second would usually be taken for granted. Frank assertion of the actual is so far a conversational norm that we can scarcely conceive of alternative incompatible adverbs: it would be very unusual for anyone to fill the slot with anything that had the sense 'not actually' or 'not frankly'. The likeliest existential paradigm for *actually* in (133) can be compared with, let us say, *usually*:

    I don't | actually | like it

             | usually |
    I don't | always | like it
             | etc.

In the light of such a representation, we have no difficulty in explaining the treatment of *usually* in:

(135) Q: Why don't you try the pâté?
     R: // *p* i <u>DON'T</u> // *r* <u>US</u>ually // *p* <u>LIKE</u> it //

One may dislike *usually*, *always*, or *sometimes*, and the respondent selects from the range of senses he/she regards as being part of the negotiated background to the conversation. Such an explanation does not seem to be applicable, however, to:

(136) // *p* i <u>DON'T</u> // *r* <u>AC</u>tually // *p* <u>LIKE</u> it //

(137) // *r* but <u>FRANK</u>ly // *p* i DON'T <u>WANT</u> to go //

The tendency to choose a referring tone for the adverbial is hardly surprising: if a speaker draws attention to the actuality of what he/she says or his/her own frankness in saying it, we should expect him/her to present it as something understood rather than as something the hearer will find newly enlightening. But what is not immediately apparent is why the adverbial is made prominent at all. What motivates the allocation of prominence to a word which patently realises no sense selection?

To answer this question we have to recall two points made earlier. One is that although prominent syllables usually realise simultaneous selections in a sense paradigm and in one or more of the intonation systems, the intonation choice(s) may sometimes be the only motive for prominence. The other is the point represented diagrammatically on an earlier page and here repeated:

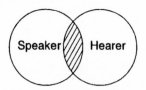

One way of interpreting this diagram is to see it as encapsulating a very obvious fact about all verbal interaction, namely that the speaker and hearer are at one and the same time *separate individuals* and *participants in some kind of social convergence*. When sense selection is associated with a referring tone, it is the location of the existential paradigm within the area of convergence that is assumed. By saying

(138) // p i <u>DON'T</u> // r <u>US</u>ually // p <u>LIKE</u> it //

a speaker articulates an assumption that a choice between *usually* and
one or more alternative adverbials is one that his/her hearer already
recognises as having significance in the ongoing business: I am drawing
attention to a distinction that *we* already know to be relevant. In
contrast, a proclaiming tone in *usually* would signify that a here-and-now
opposition between it and, say, *always*, was not yet appreciated by the
hearer; it is an opposition that only the *I* who is the speaker has so far
accommodated in his/her view of things. One way of conceptualising the
values of the choices in the P/R system is to regard them as distinguishing
between what is projected on behalf of the speaking *I* and what is
projected presumptively on behalf of the participating *we*. Seeing things
in this light enables us to separate out the meaning increments that
derive from two simultaneous selections: because of its prominence,
usually carries both a sense selection and a social connotation deriving
from the choice of referring tone, a connotation we can best describe as
an assumption of solidarity between speaker and hearer. The simultaneous selections can be represented thus:

		usually	
	(sense selection)	always	
I don't		etc.	like it
	(social selection)	togetherness	
		separateness	

Returning now to (136), where we said there would usually be no
question of there being a sense selection, we can analyse the selection
process as follows:

		actually	
I don't	(sense selection)		like it
	(social selection)	togetherness	
		separateness	

In informal conversation we make use of a number of words and
phrases like *actually* and *frankly* which, occurring characteristically with
referring tone, serve principally to insinuate a measure of generalised
intimacy or solidarity into the speaker/hearer relationship – a kind of

verbal hand-on-your-shoulder gesture. Sometimes there is a suggestion of confidentiality or conspiracy, an overtone that we can also trace to the concept of a social interpenetration of the two worlds. Everyone else is excluded, by implication, from the area of convergence: the participants' *we* excludes the non-participating *they*. Among the items used in this way are *personally*, *really* and *to tell you the truth*.

There is a complementary set of items, of which *of course, in fact, indeed* and *I can assure you* are representative, which often occur with proclaiming tone:

(139) $// p$ of COURSE $// p$ you OUGHT to be more CAREful $//$

(140) $// p$ in FACT $// p$ i HADn't yet MET him $//$

Here, too, the absence of any alternative sense selection often results in the phrase having no prominence:

(141) $// p$ of course you OUGHT to be more CAREful $//$

(142) $// p$ in fact i HADn't yet MET him $//$

When it *is* prominent, as in our earlier versions, we can see that it serves to project the generalised social implications of proclaiming tone: the speaker locates himself/herself outside the area of convergence, and foregrounds his/her own role as a non-assimilated participant in the interaction. In the two examples given above, we can say quite simply that he/she establishes his/her status as one having an independent viewpoint before going on to make his/her assertion. They both demonstrate, too, that their contribution to the discourse is quite independent of the content of the assertion he/she chose.

We have spent some time on a small number of language items whose place might be judged to be on the periphery of a description of English. The reason for doing so, and for relating them carefully to our account of the P/R opposition, is that they provide the basis for the most general characterisation of the latter. All choices in the P/R system contribute separative or associative implications to the tonic segment. Whether the tone selection is interpreted as having specific or non-specific force depends upon whether there is a simultaneous selection sense: the component of meaning we have spoken of as 'social' is always present, that attributable to a choice of sense is not.

If the last statement seems to imply an either/or situation, it is a serious oversimplification. We have chosen to exemplify two extremes of a continuum. We feel confident in saying that *usually* will more often realise a sense selection and that *actually* more often will not. We might be less confident about *incidentally* in:

(143)   // r inci<u>DEN</u>tally // p WHAT did you think of the <u>LEC</u>ture //

It is fairly common for *incidentally* to be used (with either referring or proclaiming tone) for what appear to be purely social purposes. The choice of an item for carrying consolidatory or separative meanings is to some extent a matter of personal taste or changing fashion, and any word like this, that can be treated as though it excluded no alternative, is a likely candidate. There are, however, occasions when the word is clearly intended to have a selective function. There are probably more occasions when it is not possible to say whether it is so intended or not: often there is no way of telling whether the notion of 'incidentalness' really is or is not being used as a kind of qualification upon the associated assertion, and introspection suggests that the speaker himself/herself may not be able to distinguish selective and non-selective intentions clearly. If we bring together the three representative adverbials, we can arrange them to delineate a continuum, thus:

actually ······ incidentally ······ usually

At the *actually* end we have tonic segments whose value derives entirely, or almost entirely, from the social implications of the tone choice. At the opposite end are tonic segments in which the status of the selected sense as shared or unshared is predominant. Between the two we have those whose interpretation requires the hearer to take into account to a greater or lesser degree the selectional potential of the item in the given context.

5

Tone: dominance and control

In all the examples we have used for illustration in the last chapter the speaker was represented as assigning to each tone unit either a 'falling' tone (p) or a 'fall-rise' (r). The meaning opposition which these two tones realise was explicated by relating it to the complementary states of separateness and convergence which characterise the speaker/hearer relationship at the moment each successive tone unit is spoken. It will be clear that the two terms of this meaning system are mutually defining: like 'positive' and 'negative' they constitute a closed set, together exhausting the possibilities of choice in the particular paradigm they represent. We shall have to recognise later that there are situations in which, for some reason, a speaker does not adjust his/her performance to project a putative state of understanding with his/her hearer: situations in which he/she cannot, or does not wish to, make the moment-by-moment decisions on which the distribution of referring and proclaiming tones depends. We shall leave aside these less usual circumstances for the present, however, and confine our attention to discourse produced under conditions which we will speak of loosely as 'normal interaction'. Under these conditions, all tone units have either proclaiming or referring function.

We must next recognise that the speaker has other means of marking a tone unit as proclaiming than by choosing a 'fall' and other means of marking a tone unit as referring than by choosing a 'fall-rise'. Having decided on a proclaiming tone, he/she has the option of realising it as either a 'fall' or a 'rise-fall'; having decided on a referring tone, he/she can realise it either as a 'fall-rise' or as a 'rise'. We can represent the choices that make up this part of the system diagrammatically as follows:

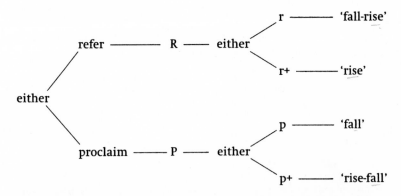

One prediction of the above diagram that we can easily test is that a 'rise-fall' can be substituted for a 'fall', and a 'rise' in any of the examples in the last chapter without disturbing the way stretches of language are presented as being within the 'common ground' or outside it. As far as this particular opposition in the meaning system is concerned, there is no difference between:

(144) $||\vee$ MARy BROWN $||\searrow$ is a TEACHer $||$ and

(145) $||\nearrow$ MARy BROWN $||\searrow$ is a TEACHer $||$

or between

(146) $||\searrow$ MARy BROWN $||\vee$ is a TEACHer $||$ and

(147) $||\wedge$ MARy BROWN $||\vee$ is a TEACHer $||$

This is not to suggest, of course, that the alternatives are likely to occur with equal frequency. The reader who tries to make the substitution in other examples may well feel that in some cases it results in somewhat improbable utterances. In others it may seem that the alternative choice fits more 'naturally' than the one on which we based the exposition in the last chapter. Such experience, as well as the probable feeling that, although the pairs that result may be similar in this particular respect, they differ in another, derives from the further selection the speaker must make, and whose meaningful consequences we must now explore.

We shall, from now on, use the transcription conventions that our diagram provides. Upper case *P* and *R* will be used when it is not necessary or helpful to distinguish between the alternative versions of each. Lower case *p* and *r* will indicate specifically the realisations of *P* and

R tones as a 'fall' and 'fall-rise' respectively. Lower case $p+$ and $r+$ will represent the alternative versions, the 'rise-fall' and the 'rise'. So, for example, the meaningful choice captured in

|| R MARy BROWN ||

will be realised in any real discourse as either

|| r MARy BROWN || or
|| r+ MARy BROWN ||

The business of this chapter is to investigate the communicative value of the feature that these conventions designate +. Having selected in the P/R system, what further significance does the speaker attach to the tonic segment by his decision to realise the selection as $p+$ rather than p, or as $r+$ rather than r?

Dominance

Once more we find ourselves having to take account of an aspect of the context of interaction. We shall begin by postulating a general condition of verbal interaction: a shared understanding of which participant is in control of the development of the discourse at any one time. This proposal may seem surprising if it is considered in relation to the apparent free-for-all of much informal conversation, and we can best clarify what we mean by attending first to those conversational events in which there are well-recognised rules governing the allocation of roles to different parties. Such events include the conventional school lesson and the doctor-patient consultation. In the former case, the right invested in the teacher, by tradition and expedience, to decide who speaks when, and to set limits to what is spoken about, makes it fairly easy to recognise him/her as occupant of what we shall call the dominant* role. Similarly, the doctor, who asks questions on which to base his/her diagnosis and eventual prescription, usually exerts overt control, discouraging irrelevances, deciding when one stage in the consultation will end and the next begin, and finally bringing it to an end. There are, of course, many other non-symmetrical verbal encounters in which the details of the role relationship are different from these. Indeed, different approaches to the business of teaching or of conducting consultations can result in what most people would regard as important differences within the patterns we have sketched in. Our present concerns are adequately served, however, if we attend to what all institutionally non-symmetrical verbal encounters have in common, and think of the common factor as an unequal distribution of conversational rights.

The particular inequality we have in mind can be described in very simple terms: in certain circumstances, which we can identify, the dominant speaker has a choice of two courses of action but, in otherwise similar circumstances, the non-dominant speaker has no such choice. Specifically, in relation to our present concern with tone, the dominant participant has the choice of either p or $p+$ tone when he/she wishes to proclaim, and of either r or $r+$ tone when he/she wishes to refer; but the non-dominant speaker must use p tone or r tone. We can illustrate this by taking a pair of utterances like:

(148) $||$ r the FIGure on the LEFT $||$ p is a TRIangle $||$

(149) $||$ $r+$ the FIGure on the LEFT $||$ p is a TRIangle $||$

While it is easy to imagine a teacher producing either of these in the course of some piece of exposition, it is unlikely that a pupil would produce the second in a response to the teacher's question.

Stating the matter in these terms does not, in itself, ascribe any kind of meaning to the act of choosing the + version in preference to the other, or vice versa. All it does is to assert that the dominant speaker is able to make a meaning distinction that the non-dominant speaker cannot make. Starting with situations in which role relationships are institutionally pre-arranged tends to obscure the fact that the assumption of a dominant role and the acceptance of a non-dominant one are, essentially, voluntary acts on the part of the speaker. Even in those encounters where there is a generally accepted prior distribution of roles, 'inferior' participants sometimes exert dominance, as most teachers and doctors would probably agree. Where there is not – in the informal conversation we spoke of earlier, for instance – it is possible and illuminating to think in terms of there being an ongoing, albeit often incipient, competition for dominance. If the + tones belong exclusively to the repertoire of the dominant speaker, then choice of a + tone at any time serves to project a context of interaction in which the speaker is dominant. For much of the time, in many conversations, role distribution is probably not an issue:

when, in the view of the speaker, it becomes an issue, conspicuous adoption of that tone whose use is reserved to the occupant of the 'superior' role externalizes his/her claim to that role.

The picture of conversational practice we have just evoked may seem to have implications of aggressiveness and other unamiable traits, implications that are not necessarily appropriate. It is true that the assumption of dominance in circumstances where there is an ongoing expectation that the speaker in question will accept a non-dominant role can sometimes amount to rudeness, but such a judgment has only local value. Once more, we have to be clear about the distinction between the generalisable meaning of the formal opposition and the precise interpretation that might be placed upon it in any one instance: the local meaning of the + option is often affected by very obscure considerations of conversational finesse. While a speaker may, on occasion, select the + option, and so project an assumption of his/her own dominance in a way which is acceptable or offensive to the hearer, we must think of this particular part of the intonation system as serving primarily to facilitate the smooth exchange of control of the discourse. The key concept in all this – control of the discourse – is the principal subject of the rest of this chapter.

The r+ tone

The data on which the description is primarily based has provided very few examples of p+ tone. Neither has informal observation of many different kinds of talk altered the impression that its use is relatively uncommon. For this reason, the dominance implication of the + element will be illustrated principally by comparing the effects of r tone and r+ tone: the tone units we shall use for exemplification will be those in which the speaker

 (i) projects an assumption of common ground, and
(ii) does or does not superimpose the increment of communicative value we have called dominance.

It is interesting to note in passing that when speakers do lay claim to the superior conversational role, they seem most often to do so at times when they are simultaneously invoking social convergence. This may be no more than an accident of sampling, and we do not wish to attach much significance to it. Others, however, have found similar relative counts of the 'rise' and the 'rise-fall' in other collections of data and it would certainly seem that the mix of meanings realised by the first would less often be disruptive of conversational harmony than might that realised by the second.

Probably the local attributes most easily ascribed to some uses of $r+$ tone in popular, common-sense language are 'forcefulness' and 'emphasis'. If we compare

(150)   // r WHEN i've finished what i'm <u>DO</u>ing // p i'll <u>HELP</u> you //

and

(151)   // r+ WHEN i've finished what i'm <u>DO</u>ing // p i'll <u>HELP</u> you //

we find that some quality of peremptoriness, or perhaps an implied determination not to help a moment *before* the speaker has finished, distinguishes the effect of the tone choice in the second version from that in the first. Paraphrases that have been suggested include:

'If you wait a minute, I'll help you,' and

'If you want me to help you, you'll have to wait.'

It may be argued that the right to keep someone waiting is, in itself, an attribute of a superior party, but the distinction we wish to highlight is that between these two locations. We can imagine a child using (150) to offer help to an adult. The use of (151) by a child might, in many circumstances, be regarded as rude. The adult, on the other hand, would normally be considered to have the choice between being accommodatingly helpful (r tone) and regulatory (r+ tone).

Compare next:

(152)   // r AFter the <u>ROUND</u>about // p we TURNED <u>LEFT</u> //

(153)   // r+ AFter the <u>ROUND</u>about // p we TURN <u>LEFT</u> //

The tone choices we have indicated for the respective items here seem to be the more probable ones, and we can usefully relate this fact to possible discourse settings. If, in (152), the speaker is apologising to his/her host for being late, and explaining how he/she lost his/her way, use of the non-dominant form seems natural enough. If, on the other hand, he/she were expostulating at having been given unsatisfactory directions, $r+$ tone could well have been chosen: it is hard to express indignation without adopting a dominant stance. If (153) is part of a sequence of directions given by a passenger to an enquiring driver – as it plausibly might be – then r+ tone is highly predictable. People placed in the position of having to give such instructions commonly adopt the intonation that marks the dominant speaker. We could say that this reflects their consciousness of the possession of desired knowledge: 'If you listen to me, I'll tell you what you want to know'. But this gloss foregrounds something that is of more central importance to us: it captures the speaker's expectation that his/her status as controller of the discourse will be recognised for the time being. Quite simply, his/her tone choice brings into the open his/her expectation that the motorist will hear him/her out until he/she has finished.

A feature of conversation that is currently attracting an increasing amount of attention is the mechanism that ensures the smooth exchange of speaker role. It is frequently observed that 'turn-taking' is usually achieved without noticeable silences or much overlapping of utterances. The factors that contribute to such exchange are complex, and involve other things than intonation. Indeed, we must immediately contradict any impression the last paragraph may have given that the choice of r+ tone necessarily means that the speaker wants to retain the initiative. The fact is, of course, that once someone has been asked to give directions everyone concerned will assume that he/she will retain speaker role until he/she has finished giving them, unless he/she temporarily relinquishes it, say by asking some such question as 'Do you know the town at all?' In order to interpret the notion of 'controlling the discourse' that we have associated with the + option in the most general way, we have to recognise cases where other factors in the situation have already determined who shall speak, but where speakers have the choice of underlining an expectation that these factors will operate. In cases like (153) it is the speaker's expectation of being allowed to continue that is underlined. Another manifestation of overt 'control', however, is the underlining of an expectation that the other party will speak. We shall now exemplify two kinds of situation in which assumption of dominance achieves two different effects. Firstly, we shall consider continuative* instances of r+ tone, where the speaker underscores his/her intention to go on. Then we shall attend to some cases where other factors independently determine that there will be a change of speaker, so that it is the expectation of a response we hear as being reinforced.

Discourse control: 1

The continuative use of r+ tone is most easily seen in a particular kind of counting-out activity. The intonation of counting has received a lot of attention, and there is a widespread feeling that a 'rising' tone is somehow the more 'natural'. Perhaps the first point to make is that counting is not, in itself, part of any kind of communicative process. To put it bluntly, few people count aloud without reference to any end that may be served by counting. To see how the activity draws upon the same meaning system as is realised by intonation in any other context, we have to think of speakers counting in the course of contributing to some conversation or other. A conceivable setting for such a conversation would be one in which a traveller has been asked to tell the customs officer how many bottles of wine he/she has in his/her luggage. His/Her answer is 'Four' and this will predictably be presented as a proclaimed tone unit: // p FOUR //. The traveller may, however, find it necessary to convince the customs officer by counting them visibly. The counting is then a shared activity, so that a referring tone is appropriate for each of the separate steps that are taken towards the required total. Counting *can* be done with non-dominant referring tone, but is then inclined to suggest deference, or even timidity, as if the counter were wanting the hearer's approval of each step he/she takes: each step might, in fact, elicit a concurring *yes*. With the more probable r+ tone, the traveller is heard as taking the business of demonstrating how many there are firmly in his/her own hands, with an intimation to the customs officer to stand back, as it were, and keep attending until he/she has finished:

(154) || r+ ONE || r+ TWO || r+ THREE || p FOUR ||

It is worth noticing that if this process fails to carry the desired conviction, the traveller might then say, in exasperation

(155) || p ONE || p TWO || p THREE || p FOUR ||

ostentatiously *telling* him/her what he/she seems unwilling to perceive. We can, furthermore, imagine the roles reversed and suppose that the customs officer, having been told that there are four bottles, insists on counting them himself/herself. As he/she produces them from the travelling bag, we might expect:

(156) $||\,r+\underline{\text{ONE}}\,||\,r+\underline{\text{TWO}}\,||\,r+\underline{\text{THREE}}\,||\,r+\underline{\text{FOUR}}\,||\,\ldots$
$||\,p\,\underline{\text{FIVE}}\,||\,p\,\underline{\text{SIX}}\,||\,p\,\underline{\text{SEV}}\text{en}\,||\,\ldots$

Here, the shared understanding is that the counting will go as far as *four*, and it is consistent with the officer's having taken control that he/she uses the dominant version of referring tone. Each addition to *four* is proclaimed because he/she is now telling the traveller of bottles that were not accounted for in the latter's declaration: the fifth and subsequent ones lie outside the area of understanding that he/she has so far accepted.

It would, of course, be possible to propose other combinations of discourse conditions and intonation choices for the encounter we have just invented. We have gone far enough, however, to establish two points. One is that the communicative value of the various intonation choices is the same in the context of 'counting' activities as in all other contexts: judgments about the 'naturalness' of 'rising' tone are really assumptions about the kind of setting we automatically make when we think of 'counting' as a phenomenon in the abstract. The other is that there is no easy way of relating 'rising' tone to a concept of 'incompleteness'. The completeness of the list depends, in our examples above, on extra-linguistic reality: the number of bottles of wine the traveller is trying to import. Each of the tones *r*, *r+* and *p* can occur at a point before the closing of the list, in accordance with the normal rules governing their distribution. If 'incompleteness' helps at all, it seems to be because the exercise of dominance prerogative often carries with it a local meaning we can make explicit as something like 'Wait for it . . .'. It is essential, however, to see this effect as deriving from the basically social value of the tone choice – the kind of context of interaction that the tone unit projects – and not see the tone choice as a reflex of the fact that the utterance might, or might not, be adjudged 'complete' on some other criteria.

Counting aloud is, perhaps, less common in life than books about intonation would lead one to suppose, and we can make the same point in relation to the more pervasive phenomenon 'syntactic incompleteness'. It is tempting to connect the 'rising' tone in

(157) $||\,r+\text{WHEN you }\underline{\text{SEE}}\text{ him}\,||\,p\,\underline{\text{ASK}}\text{ him}\,||$

with the fact that the *when*-clause does not end this particular sentence.

This explanation breaks down immediately we reverse the constituents, however:

(158) $||$ p ASK him $||$ r+ WHEN you SEE him $||$

We have seen, moreover, in Chapter 4 that the tone choices in both these examples are reversible, in so far as the referring and proclaiming increments of value are concerned. Over and above the distribution of referring and proclaiming tones, all that needs to be explained is what motivates the choice of the + version of the former. Our examples seem, in fact, to make this choice the more likely one: the kind of speaker/ hearer relationship that sanctions use of imperative mood would often be the kind in which the speaker would signal overtly an assumption of dominant role. But the fact that one *could* use r tone in otherwise identical utterances makes it clear that using imperative clauses and making overt one's control of the discourse result from quite separate speaker-decisions. Something can be learnt from a consideration of how referring tones are realised at the ends of syntactic sentences – at points, that is, where the criteria of 'syntactic incompleteness' could not apply. Consider:

(159) Speaker A: What time does the heating come on?

Speaker B: $||$ p there $\underline{IS}$n't any heating $||$ r on SATurdays $||$

With referring tone in the last tone unit of his/her utterance Speaker B would probably be heard as making an adequate response to A and as having nothing more to say on the matter. If we substitute r+ tone, there is a strong expectation that there is more to follow:

(160) $||$ p there $\underline{IS}$n't any heating $||$ r+ on SATurdays $||$ p it's PART of

the e$\underline{CON}$omy drive $||$

We can say that, in ending one sentence, and thus coming to a point where it might be thought that the utterance would finish, Speaker B foreshadows his/her intention of starting another one by underlining his/ her present status as controller of the discourse: there is an overlaid warning to 'wait for it'. Pointing out another possibility will serve as a warning against applying an over-simple explanation. It could be that if Speaker B said

(161) // p there $\underline{IS}$n't any heating // r+ on $\underline{SAT}$urdays //

and accompanied it with a clear indication that he/she did *not* intend to go on, a turn towards A or an expectant and mystified look might then be sufficient to pass the speaker-role back again. The effect of the controlling element in the tone choice would now be to increase the pressure upon Speaker A to comment. The local interpretation might be something like 'You know perfectly well there isn't!' or 'Do you think we're rolling in money?' The surprise, or reproach, which would not have been made overt in the same way if r tone had been chosen derives from the compulsion A is now expected to feel to say something by way of explanation for his/her inappropriate question.

We have said that syntax and non-vocal features might be instrumental in determining whether there is a change of speaker or not, and that diametrically opposed manifestations of discourse control – the meanings 'wait' and 'go on' – attach to r+ tones, depending on how these other features are interpreted. Before going on to illustrate the second sort, we will consider a verbal activity that exemplifies clearly, and often *in extenso*, what we have called the continuative implication: the telling of stories.

The following will be recognised, in their manner of presentation, as typical of a certain kind of story-telling:

(162) // r+ a GREAT while a$\underline{GO}$ // r+ while there were STILL $\underline{GI}$ants on
the earth // . . .

(163) // r+ THIS chap i $\underline{KNEW}$ // p he'd JUST got a new $\underline{JOB}$ // r+ and
the VERy first $\underline{DAY}$ // . . .

It is an underlying assumption of much story-telling that for most of the time hearers are being asked to recall an already shared tradition rather than being told anything new. In the adult anecdote suggested by (163) we can imagine some such continuation as

. . . // r+ and the VERy first $\underline{DAY}$ // r+ he'd GOT there nice and
EARly // r+ and he was JUST taking his $\underline{COAT}$ off // r+ and
TRYing to look $\underline{KEEN}$ // . . .

in which the teller evokes, detail by detail, a stereotypical situation. There is a knowing implication that 'we' all know what the first day in a new job is like. Against the background of such familiar detail, the teller introduces the first step towards whatever point the story is eventually going to have. The preponderantly evocative effect of a narrative that makes such extensive use of referring tones can best be appreciated by comparing it with a certain kind of written narrative. A sensible reading of the following seems to demand exclusive use of proclaiming tones:

(164) // p he <u>FELT</u> // p some DARK <u>PRES</u>ence // p MOVing irresistibly up<u>ON</u> him // p from the <u>DARK</u>ness // p a presence <u>SUB</u>tle // p and MURmurous as a <u>FLOOD</u> // p FILling him <u>WHOL</u>ly // p with it<u>SELF</u> //

Here, the narrator recreates, detail by detail, a cumulative experience; and as each detail is represented as impinging freshly upon his/her consciousness, so the hearer is made to feel that each detail is a new incursion into *his/her* world view. But if insinuated togetherness, of the kind that is suggested by (163), is one characteristic of anecdote-swapping sessions, another characteristic is their open competitiveness; and this would seem to account for the usual realisation of referring tones as r+. The teller must not only establish his/her position *as* teller at the beginning, but continuously reiterate his/her claim to dominant status – repeatedly insist on his/her expectation to be allowed to go on uninterrupted – until the end. The same mechanisms work, to essentially the same effect, in the nursery story. The formulae 'A great while ago . . .' and 'Once upon a time . . .' occur most often with rising tone, and serve among other functions to indicate that the speaker is at this moment assuming the story-teller's control of subsequent verbal behaviour. The going over of well-known material, with spaces left for the listening child to fill

(165) // r+ <u>FATH</u>er bear // r+ <u>MOTH</u>er bear // and . . .

would seem to represent a particularly open exercise of that control.

Discourse control: 2

To begin our investigation of cases where dominance is manifested as a pressure upon the other party to speak, we will compare the effect of tone choice in:

(166) // r is THIS the SHEFfield train //

(167) // r+ is THIS the SHEFfield train //

We have not yet said anything about the significance of choices in the P/R system in interrogative items like these. There are certain problems in the interpretation of the 'common ground' metaphor we have used, problems that will be examined in the next chapter. The reason for postponing it until then is that in some circumstances referring tone is more typically realised as r+ than as r in such items, and it seemed better to consider first why this should be the case.

Assuming, then, that we can find a motive for choosing a version of referring tone in (166) and (167), we have to ask what are the effects of choosing one rather than the other. A first answer to the question might be that (166) avoids overt assumption of superiority in the encounter. The consequence is an enquiry which can be heard as 'polite' or 'diffident'; or even as a request for the favour of a reply. Version (167) contrasts with this, sounding more like the utterance of someone who demands the information as of right. Its peremptoriness, or brusqueness, might well make it unacceptable in many circumstances. It would be reasonable to try to relate the choice in this particular example to the relatively permanent relationship existing between the participants. We might, for instance, expect the first if the speaker were addressing a fellow-traveller but the second if he/she were speaking to a railway official. This is quickly seen, however, to be altogether too simple an equation: considerations of politeness to public servants, or of not adopting an overbearing manner, would usually complicate things. The general explanation we have proposed requires that we take account, not of institutionalised relationships as such, but of the immediate, here-and-now stance that the speaker adopts as a participant in the interaction. We have to consider the combined effect of the speaker simultaneously using an interrogative form and making claim to control the discourse by adopting dominant role. Obviously, our question sets up some expectation that the other participant will continue, no matter which of the tones is chosen. It is not suggested that the expectation will be any greater or any less as a result of the tone choice. What we do have to recognise is that the speaker has the option of underpinning his/her role as the person who is determining what happens next at the same time as he/she makes a request for information.

The difference between the two versions is simply whether his/her attempt to exercise control over what the other person does by asking a question is, or is not, accompanied by the intonation feature that draws attention to what he/she is doing.

We said above that the overt assumption of dominance in this situation might possibly give offence, and we can go a little further towards characterising the effects of the r/r+ choice if we examine the circumstances in which it seems more socially acceptable to use the one rather than the other. A useful rough distinction can be made between questions that are asked for the benefit of the speaker and those that are asked for the benefit of the hearer. In the following, we should usually say that the hearer was the proposed beneficiary:

(168)   // R CAN i HELP you //

Choice of r+ tone here would probably result in this being heard as a warmer offer than if r tone were chosen. Overt control of the response would be taken as a more wholehearted attempt to have the offer accepted. By selecting r tone the speaker might run the risk of suggesting a merely routine or desultory interest in giving help. For comparison, the question realised as either (166) or (167) above is almost certain to lead to an outcome of advantage to the enquirer: when this is the case, it is the r+ version that runs the greater risk of displeasing. Both realisations are common in utterances like

(169)   // R have you FINished //   and

(170)   // R are you READy //

but with markedly different effects depending upon who stands to gain. If either of them is a conversational surrogate for 'Can I help you to a second serving?' the r+ version is more pressing and cordial. If, on the other hand, it has the force of something like 'I've been waiting for you', overt dominance introduces a superimposed note of irritation or exasperation into the relationship.

If it is true, as random observation tends to suggest, that questions are more frequently associated with a 'rising' tone than with a 'fall-rise', the reason is to be sought in the subtly-adjusted role-expectations that characterise the settings in which questions are asked. It does not, on the surface of it, seem improbable that questions are asked more often by people who are in open occupancy of the dominant role than by people who are not.

Reminding

We will briefly consider one other effect of the exercise of conversational dominance. Both r tone and r+ tone occur in the following, in virtually identical circumstances:

(171) Speaker A: // p i WONder who'll <u>COME</u> //
       Speaker B: // r well <u>TOM</u> will // r and <u>MAR</u>y // r+ and <u>JANE</u> // . . .

Choice of referring tone for *Tom*, *Mary* and *Jane*, implies that all three are members of the group who Speaker A already knows will come: whether for tactical or other reasons, Speaker B refers to their likely appearance as already negotiated common ground. What distinguishes the presentation of *Jane* from that of the other two is the implication that A may have temporarily forgotten her. The relevant distinction seems to be that between matter which is not only common ground but also vividly present in the consciousness of the hearer and common-ground matter which the speakers assume they need to reactivate. To put it another way, the speakers act as though the hearer's diagram of the present state of convergence

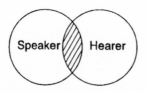

were different from his/her own. We have insisted that it is always open to a speaker to insinuate convergence in such circumstances: our speaker could have treated Jane like the other two, but to do so would, in some sense, be to perpetrate a fiction. What results from the assumption of dominance is the open recognition that B needs reminding: one aspect of discourse control is the ability to intervene and redraw the convergence map of the interaction, and by adopting r+ tone one can make clear that he/she is making such an intervention.

p+ tone

The little we have to say about the combination of dominance with proclaiming tone can be best related to the last section. If discourse control includes the ability to decide how the world view of speaker and hearer are to be regarded as relating, this means that it includes the ability of the speaker to modify his/her own world view as external events impinge upon him/her. With use of the non-dominant *p* tone, there is no way of knowing whether

(172) // *p* it's RAINing //

proclaims news that the speaker had known for some time, or whether it is something that has only just been noticed. With *p+* tone the speaker is heard as proclaiming the fact at the very moment of discovering it for himself/herself: typically, we should expect such an utterance as he/she looks out through the window. Again, the open indication that he/she is using the dominant speaker's prerogative to change the state of his/her world – and hence the map that accommodates the worlds of both speaker and hearer – gives the utterance its particular local meaning:

(173) // *p+* it's RAINing // (= 'Who'd have thought it!')

In saying – as popular usage encourages us to say – that such an utterance is 'exclamatory', we are recognising the extent to which it is isolated, both grammatically and discoursally, from any surrounding verbal activity. People do not normally feel the need to respond to an exclamation 'It's raining!' in the way they might to the comment 'It's raining'. This is another way of saying that choice of the dominant tone makes manifest the speaker's intention of controlling the discourse: he/she registers his/her *own* observation that it is raining and simultaneously indicates that he/she expects no feedback of either an adjudicating or a concurring kind. The same is even more transparently true of expostulations like

(174) // *p+* REALly // , // *p+* GRACious // , // *p+* my DEAR FELlow //

which we might paraphrase as 'What you have just said, or done, astonishes me (that is to say, it changes my world view), and I am registering my surprise in a way which assumes that *you* will not participate in it'. We need not dwell on the fact that blasphemies and obscenities used in a similar way constitute a kind of withdrawal from whatever verbal interaction may be in progress – we customarily swear to ourselves rather than at the other party, and the option of doing this is patently vested in the dominant speaker.

Most of the $p+$ tones encountered in data or noticed in overheard speech have been in situations where dominance serves to mark the here-and-now modification of the speaker's world view. As we said earlier, this may be an accident. Certainly we can construct examples in which the controlling implication we have associated with the + factor works in the more general way to either inhibit or encourage immediate speaker-change. The continuative implication is exemplified by:

(175)   Speaker A: He's clever, isn't he?
        Speaker B: $||\,p\,\underline{\text{YES}}\,||$

(176)   Speaker A: He's clever, isn't he?
        Speaker B: $||\,p+\underline{\text{YES}}\,||\,p$ he $\underline{\text{IS}}\,||$

In (175) it is not difficult to imagine the second speaker contenting himself/herself with a concurring *yes* and waiting for the first speaker to go on. In (176), the choice of the dominant version for the concurrence signals the second speaker's intention to go on. We might say that, locally, the treatment of *yes* results in its being heard as a more enthusiastic concurrence, but it is easy to show that this is because of the reiteration, '. . . he is', that it seems to prefigure. The intimation, 'I have more to say', may, however, have a quite different fulfilment:

(177) $||\,p+\underline{\text{YES}}\,||\,p$ but DOESn't he $\underline{\text{KNOW}}$ it $||$

For the other effect of the + element, we will compare interrogative items having proclaiming tones:

(178) $||\,p\,\text{WHY}$ don't you $\underline{\text{ASK}}$ him $||$

(179) $||\,p+\text{WHY}$ don't you $\underline{\text{ASK}}$ him $||$

As in the case of the questions that had referring tones, we can say that both invite a response, but the addition of something we might perhaps characterise locally as 'forcefulness' or 'insistence' can be traced to the fact that the speaker overtly assumes dominant-speaker status.

6

Tone: questions and social elicitation

In this chapter we shall retrace our steps a little in order to deal with a range of uses of proclaiming and referring tone that have so far been largely ignored. These are their uses in connection with what we will provisionally call interrogative function. Intonation manuals have given a great deal of attention to what they describe as the intonation of questions; and probably the idea that there is something one can identify without difficulty as 'questioning intonation' has wider currency outside the professional worlds of language teaching and linguistic study than anything else pertaining to the subject matter of this book.

There are two principal reasons why we have put off examining the significance of the P/R opposition in this much discussed set of contexts until now. One is that it seemed best to give some account of the basis on which the precise realisation of a proclaiming or referring tone is chosen. We are prepared now for the likelihood that in many of the examples in this chapter, the choice signified by the generalising symbol R will seem to be more naturally realised *either* as r tone *or* as r+ tone, the particular version being dependent on considerations of projected role relationships that are not directly relevant to the discussion in which we shall engage. The other reason is that the metaphorical apparatus that has sufficed so far, involving notions of common ground and the conversational pursuit of speaker/hearer convergence, will require some revision if it is to be applied to interrogative contexts.

'Declarative-mood' questions

A necessary first step is to distinguish between interrogative grammar – the basis on which 'questions' are most commonly held to be identifiable – and a special function of the utterance – also usually regarded as having interrogative implications – whose characterisation can only be framed adequately in terms of some account of discourse structure. As a start, we can consider the following pair of utterances:

(a)   I prefer that one

(b)   You prefer that one?

The question mark appended to (b) reflects the probability that, declarative mood notwithstanding, the speaker will not be telling the hearer about his/her (that is the hearer's) own preference. He/She is more likely to be asking the hearer to respond to the tentative assertion he/she makes. The invited response will then be concurrence, if mid termination is chosen, or adjudication, if termination is high. Assuming that all other variables remain constant, we can say that the discourse values of (a) and (b) are determined on the basis of who knows what. If we now add a further example

(c)   John prefers that one (?)

the appropriacy or inappropriacy of the question mark will depend on whether it is the speaker or the hearer who is privy to John's preferences. In all three cases, the discourse function of the utterance depends crucially on the state of understanding existing between speaker and hearer. While in the cases of (a) and (b), inherent probability serves as a fair (but by no means infallible) guide to what that understanding is, in that of (c) only additional knowledge, derived from the text or from elsewhere, would enable the analyst to know what function was intended. Indeed, the understanding may be less complete than the speaker takes it to be: we hear dialogues like:

Speaker A: John prefers that one
Speaker B: Does he?
Speaker A: I'm asking you!

The significance of tone choice has to be examined against a background of these (non-intonational) facts.

It is evident that if proclaiming tone is selected with examples (a) and (b)

(180)   // p I prefer THAT one //

(181)   // p YOU prefer THAT one //

only the first can be explained in the way proposed in Chapter 4. If we regard both as tending towards the removal of some kind of uncertainty on the part of one of the participants, the purpose of (b) must be seen as the removal of the speaker's uncertainty, not the hearer's. The world-changing element is not the assertion, but the *yes* (or *no*) that it seeks to elicit. The modification we have to make to our conceptual apparatus is to regard the step towards convergence that the speaker initiates as being brought about by the response it pre-empts. So, too, in the two, situationally-conditioned, interpretations of

(182) // *p* JOHN prefers <u>THAT</u> one //

the speaker either offers to change the hearer's world view or articulates an assumption that the latter will change *his/her* world view, depending on the existing context of interaction.

Examples similar to all these could occur with referring tone. Changes in the distribution of prominence and the specification of particular choices of *r* tone and *r+* tone will make them easier to contextualise but will not otherwise affect the present argument:

(183) // *r* i pre<u>FER</u> that one // (but I can't afford it)

(184) // *r+* you preFER <u>THAT</u> one // (Is that what you're saying?)

(185) // *r* john pre<u>FERS</u> that one // (He told me so)

(186) // *r+* JOHN pre<u>FERS</u> that one // (Is that what you're saying?)

Examples (183) and (185) are both accounted for by what was said about referring tone in Chapter 4: both project a context of interaction in which the content of the referring tone unit is common ground. Examples (184) and (186) similarly present their matter as if it were understanding already negotiated. Here, however, we might normally feel that the speaker was not strictly in a position to present it in this way; because of the likely distribution of knowledge, the speaker is now heard as proferring a tentative assessment of common ground and asking the hearer to concur with, or adjudicate with respect to, its validity: 'Am I right in thinking – that is to say, am I right in taking it as already established between us – that . . . ?' As in the case of the interrogative item with proclaiming tone, a step towards greater convergence is achieved only with the production of the following response, but now it is an area of common ground provisionally mapped out by the speaker that awaits the confirmation of a proclaimed endorsement, *yes* (or *no*).

There may not seem to be very much to choose between presenting a possible truth and asking to have it confirmed or refuted (which is a rough way of saying what the proclaimed versions (181) and (182) do) and the alternative (represented by the referring versions (184) and (186)) of making a provisional assessment of what can be taken to be negotiated and asking to have *that* confirmed or refuted. Certainly there are occasions when it is difficult to attribute sharply distinguished local consequences to the fact that one option has been taken up rather than the other. Once more, to give conceptual substance to the value of the formal choice, we must have recourse to looking at situations where that value becomes apparent. We will proceed then, on the assumption that certain declarative-mood items function as questions because of the prevailing state of speaker/hearer understanding, and that they serve to elicit a response which, if forthcoming, will remove some kind of uncertainty from the mind of the speaker.

As an illustration of how the mechanism works with referring tone, consider:

(187) // r you're GOing OUT //

Addressed to someone who was in the act of buttoning up his/her overcoat, this can be interpreted as a presentation of the apparent intentions of the hearer as if they were negotiated common ground and a simultaneous request for confirmation: 'Please confirm that I am drawing the right conclusions from your actions'. With proclaiming tone, on the other hand, the utterance projects a context in which the speaker does not know what interpretation to put on the hearer's conduct:

(188) // p you're GOing OUT //
       ('Is *that* it? Or if not, what *are* you going to do?')

Consider next:

(189) Speaker A: // p i've JUST been talking to JOHN //
       Speaker B: // r you've BEEN in the OFfice //
       Speaker A: // p YES //

Here, Speaker B's assumption of what may be taken for common ground is based not upon visual evidence but upon A's preceding assertion. With proclaiming tone, however,

(190) $|| p$ you've BEEN in the OFfice $||$

would propose one of the possible places where *John* could have been encountered but with the implication that, for all the speaker knows, it might have been elsewhere: 'Is *that* what you're telling me?'

Special interest attaches to examples like the following:

(191) Speaker A: $|| p$ i SAW him in OXford street $||$
         Speaker B: $|| r$ you SAW him in OXford street $||$
         Speaker A: $|| p$ YES $||$

In both (187) and (189) the declarative mood item with referring tone serves to check an inference. Such an explanation clearly cannot be applied to Speaker B's contribution to (191). We can take it that when a speaker echoes the lexis and grammar of an utterance like this, the appropriate paraphrase is not 'Am I right in concluding . . .' but rather something like 'Am I right in thinking you said (and meant) . . .'. The local effect of such an echo could often be described in terms of surprise: 'Have I heard (understood) you correctly?' usually indicates that what has been heard is in some way contrary to expectations. Provided we retain mid key, an otherwise identical proclaimed version lacks this element of expectation.

(192) $|| p$ you SAW him in OXford street $||$

has no implications of 'That's an odd place for him to be!' It might, perhaps, follow A's assertion made in the course of a police enquiry, where the questioner was making absolutely sure that the witness had remembered accurately. By projecting a situation in which all the other assertions A might have made are regarded as still possible, the interrogator says, in effect: 'Think again – was it Oxford Street, or was it somewhere else?' Similarly, we may compare the effect of tone choice in the doctor's utterance in:

(193) Doctor: $|| p$ where do you GET this pain $||$
       Patient: $|| p$ in my HEAD $||$
       Doctor: $|| p/r+$ you GET it in your HEAD $||$
       Patient: $|| p$ YES $||$

For the doctor to choose referring tone would probably be alarming to the patient: by seeming to question his/her own hearing or understanding of what the latter has said, he/she would give the impression that he/she has never known anyone have this particular kind of pain *there* before! With proclaiming tone he/she would be heard as asking for greater precision – a recycling of the question so to speak – by behaving as though the patient had not yet selected a response, and leading perhaps to 'Yes. Behind my eyes'.

The interpretation of the last few examples is complicated by the fact that both referring and proclaiming tones combine with high and mid termination, and in each case there can be alternative meanings traceable to the latter choice. The difficulty of keeping the effects of the two systems separate in some cases is well demonstrated by a re-examination of (191). We saw that choice of referring tone in the echo signified uncertainty about whether the speaker had heard correctly. But notice that simultaneous choice of proclaiming tone and high termination can sometimes justify a very similar local interpretation:

(194)   // p you SAW him in <u>OX</u>ford street //
        (= 'Is that, or is it not, what you said (meant)?')

Surprise or incredulity can easily be attributed to both. Probably the highest degree of incredulity attaches, however, to the combination of high termination *and* referring tone. The way the effects of these two choices combine, and the way they relate to other combinations can be summarised as follows:

	mid termination	high termination
referring tone	1 This is what I infer, or think I heard. Please confirm that I am right.	2 This is what I infer, or think I heard. Please tell me whether I am right or not.
proclaiming tone	3 Can I infer, or did you say (mean), this or something else? Please confirm that it was *this*.	4 Can I infer, or did you say (mean), this or something else? Please tell me whether *this* is right or not.

Allowing for the unavoidable clumsiness and approximateness of paraphrase, it is evident from this that no particular intonation choice and
no special combination of choices can be identified as specifically an
interrogative intonation. Why, then, is it so commonly said that it can?
One reason that suggests itself is that combination 3 in our table is likely
to be fairly uncommon in most kinds of discourse. To exemplify its use,
we have been driven to proposing contexts in which police officers and
doctors are being especially careful about the collection of facts. Occasions for this kind of care are comparatively rare in other contexts,
where we may therefore suppose that the other three combinations are
more commonly associated with declarative mood elicitations. Two of
these have a 'rising' tone in their dominant versions and a 'fall-rise' in
their non-dominant versions. The last has high termination. Although we
have separated the first two from the last as quite distinct formal
choices, the fact that there is a phonetically high peak somewhere near
the end of both kinds of tone unit seems to have caused serious
confusion in much of what has been said and written in a non-technical
way about how questions rise at the end. No doubt the confusion has
been encouraged by the similarity in local effects that we have noted.

Yes/no questions

A full discussion of the difference between

(a)   You prefer that one? and

(b)   Do you prefer that one?

would take us further into matters of discourse organisation than it
would be appropriate to go here. Fortunately, there is little need to
engage in such a discussion. It is sufficient for present purposes to note
that considerations of who knows what about whose intentions are
located in the unique conversational nexus we have called the context of
interaction. We can take it that the significance of the grammatical form
of (b) is that it marks the utterance as interrogative even in the absence
of any relevant features of speaker/hearer understanding: 'Does he prefer
that one?' is unambiguously interrogative in situations where the value
of 'He prefers that one' might well be in doubt. Once this measure of

similarity has been recognised, we can go on to show that the value of either tone choice in the P/R system in (b) is essentially the same as the value that same choice has in (a). Compare:

(195) // p DO you prefer <u>THAT</u> one //

(196) // r+DO you prefer <u>THAT</u> one //

The communicative value of (195) is predictably something like: 'I don't know whether you do or not – please tell me', while that of (196) is something like: 'Am I right in assuming you do?' Once more, however, it is necessary to imagine some more-or-less precisely specified speech situations in order to separate out meanings which may often seem, for all practical purposes, to fall together in their local implications.

Certain kinds of guessing game provide plenty of examples of questions like:

(197) // p IS it an <u>EL</u>ephant //

The form of our transcription indicates that there are two sense selections in this utterance, and therefore two matters with respect to which the speaker might be declaring his uncertainty. The following representation of conceivable existential paradigms will help to clarify:

			elephant
	is		
It		an	alligator
	isn't		
			armadillo

We can take this representation as revealing an ambiguity that inheres in the printed item. The speaker may be seeking to determine whether it *is* or *is not* an elephant, or he/she may want to know whether it is an elephant or something else. Depending upon which of the interpretations is judged to be the appropriate one, a concurring *yes* will have the meaning 'Yes, it is' or 'Yes, an elephant'.

A series of guesses might go:

(198) // p IS it an <u>EL</u>ephant // . . . // p IS it an arma<u>DIL</u>lo // . . . // p or a <u>POR</u>cupine // . . .

At the beginning of a 'round', participants are often in a position where genuine guessing is the only way forward: *elephant*, *armadillo* and *porcu-pine* are selections from a set which is limited only by whatever conventions the game happens to have. The players may know, for instance, that the object is necessarily animal rather than vegetable or mineral, or that it begins with a particular letter of the alphabet, but otherwise the possibilities are entirely open. Often, the question-master's rejection of incorrect offers will show his/her understanding of this: 'No, not an elephant'.

In most games of this kind, however, one can expect that after guessing or random elimination has proceeded for a whole, the field will be sufficiently narrowed for players to make a more-or-less informed prediction of what the sought-for object might be. At this point, scientific deduction or hunch might suggest that *alligator* is a candidate worthy of being put forward as a likely winner, not just as a hopeful selection. The question-master is now asked, in effect, to concur with the proposal 'It's an alligator': 'Yes, it is'. Observation suggests that while players present their guesses with proclaiming tones, they present their deductions or hunches with referring tones. Furthermore, if the supply of intelligent offers runs out before they get the right answer, they characteristically mark their return to guessing by reverting to proclaiming tone.

These observations cannot, of course, be verified point by point in any particular sample of data. There is no way of establishing independently whether players are guessing or not, and they can in any case decide for themselves to disguise their wildest guesses as judicious deductions and vice-versa. Moreover, in frequently repeated routines like panel games, ritualised patterns of behaviour can easily replace the kind of situation-sensitive tone choices we have described. There is nevertheless sufficient reason for saying that such activities illustrate in a more-than-usually transparent way the operation of the P/R opposition in conjunction with yes/no elicitations, an operation that we can now describe as follows. With proclaiming tone, the speaker asks for the removal of uncertainty with respect to one of a number of existentially possible options: he/she projects a context in which the response is so far un-negotiated and, trying out one of the options, offers it for the hearer to concur with or reject. Concurrence or rejection will, it is acknowledged, alter the speaker's world view. With referring tone, the speaker tentatively projects a context in which the response has been negotiated: all he/she asks of a respondent is confirmation (or denial) that the assumption he/she is making about the common ground is the proper one. We may say that he/she modifies his/her world view *in advance* and submits the modification for the hearer's approval.

Both referring and proclaiming tones are possible in the second speaker's contribution in:

(199) Speaker A: I wish I could remember his name!
      Speaker B: // r/p IS it <u>AR</u>thur //

The alternative local values are different from those we have just examined, but they are traceable to the same general opposition. With proclaiming tone, Speaker B will probably be heard as rather unhelpfully suggesting a name off the top of his/her head. With referring tone, *Arthur* is proposed as being sufficiently probable to make it worthwhile considering whether it is the forgotten name: 'I think it might be Arthur – am I right?' Such a response might, for instance, fit a situation where both participants know that there is someone named Arthur connected with the ongoing business in some way. It is, of course, part of the projected assumption that Speaker A will recognise the information as having been already negotiated once it is proposed. Keeping in mind that a mid-termination choice would simultaneously signal the expectation of a concurring *yes*, we can see why referring tone versions of items like this often sound like reminders – like reinvocations of common ground temporarily forgotten.

In a further example

(200) // p WILL you have <u>COF</u>fee //

a proclaimed version suggests either one of a range of things the hearer might care to drink:

	coffee
Will you have	tea
	etc.

or perhaps, one of a range of things he/she might care to do (take a bath, go for a walk, etc.). The version with referring tone

(201) // R WILL you have <u>COF</u>fee //

takes the obvious availability of *coffee* for granted and politely projects the assumption that the other person will have some. There is no implication that there is a choice, nor is the respondent put in the position of having to make a decision which will be world-changing for his/her host; the guest is asked only to concur with a proposal that the latter presents *as if* the taking of coffee had already been settled.

In some settings it is hard to imagine yes/no elicitations having the kind of interpretation we have associated with proclaiming tones. At the dental surgery we might hear

(202) Patient: I have an appointment for two o'clock.
       Receptionist: // r are YOU mister ROBinson //

the receptionist being concerned only to check his/her assumption that the person addressing him/her is the one whose name is in his/her appointments book. With proclaiming tone, the same enquiry might suggest, rather worryingly, that the arrangements were in such a mess that he/she didn't know *who* to expect next. In

(203) Speaker A: I can't find my book.
       Speaker B: // r IS it robinson CRUsoe //

the second speaker checks that the lost book *is* the one he/she saw earlier in the day before saying something like: 'I think it's in the bathroom'. There would seem to be considerably less likelihood of him/her having seen several open books about the house and having to discover which belonged to Speaker A before making a suggestion. Similarly, the example we used in the last chapter

(204) // r is THIS the SHEFfield train //

would usually serve to check a presumption that it was, since the traveller having normally consulted a timetable or taken some other steps beforehand to ensure that he/she was on the right platform at the right time.

It is probably because situations like those we have just glanced at are more typical of those in which questions of this grammatical type are asked that it is so often asserted that rising tones are in some way the more natural accompaniment of the yes/no elicitation. Without entering into any arithmetical comparison, we can recognise that we do, more often than not, direct enquiry to a yes/no choice in circumstances where askers have some reason – substantive or tactical – for projecting an assumption that they know the answer. Guessing, and such like activities, which represent eliciting in unnegotiated situations, are less frequent in most kinds of discourse. The point to be emphasised, however, is that any statistical probability of pairing between tone choice and grammatical type reflects nothing more than the kinds of situation in which yes/no elicitations tend to occur. While it is obviously of great interest, it should not be allowed to obscure the fact that the choice of referring or proclaiming tone rests on the same kind of consideration as it does in any other grammatical environment. All that is necessary is to adjust our conceptual schema – the use we make, for instance, of the 'common ground' metaphor – to take account of which of the participants' world views is subject to change.

Information questions

An exactly parallel approach will enable us to account for the significance of the P/R opposition in relation to information elicitations of the type: 'Where's the elephant?' In this case, however, it is easier to imagine speakers seeking information that they have no reason to represent as having been already negotiated. The existential paradigm for the item in the response that replaces the interrogative *where* might have a considerable number of members:

Where's the elephant?	In the paddock
	Over there
	Behind the aviary
	etc.

The longstanding tradition that 'falling' tone occurs with an elicitation of this type

(205) // p WHERE'S the ELephant //

recognises just such an open situation as this. But we can easily show that it is not the only kind of situation in which information elicitations are produced. Consider:

(206) Speaker A: I can't find my book.
　　　 Speaker B: // r WHAT'S it <u>CALLED</u> //

With referring tone in his/her utterance, Speaker B is heard as asking, not for information about which of the many titles the book might have it actually carried on its cover, but rather whether it is the book he/she recently saw in the bathroom or elsewhere. There is, in fact, a close similarity between what he/she says and:

(207) // r IS it robinson <u>CRU</u>soe //

The two anticipate different responses: 'Robinson Crusoe' in the case of (206), and 'Yes' in the case of (207). But they both further the business of finding the lost book by checking B's provisional assumption about what book it is before he/she goes on to make a suggestion as to where it might be found. If we substitute a proclaiming tone in (206)

(208) // p WHAT'S it <u>CALLED</u> //

we get an implication of openness with respect to the title very similar to that we found with the yes/no elicitation: 'Tell me the title, so that I shall recognise it if I come across it'.

Compare also:

(209) // p WHAT <u>TIME</u> is it //

(210) // r WHAT <u>TIME</u> is it //

While (209) projects a context of interaction in which a respondent is expected to select from a set of possible times, (210) characteristically has the kind of checking function that might otherwise be realised with a yes/no elicitation like: 'Is it as late as I think it is?' or 'Isn't it time we were leaving?'

In the last section we noted some situations in which it seemed unlikely that yes/no elicitations would occur with proclaiming tone. It follows from the argument we are now developing that there will often be an information elicitation that serves much the same end provided it has referring tone, and that the imagined discourse conditions will make a proclaimed version of this equally improbable. We can check this:

(211) Patient: I have an appointment for two o'clock.
　　　 Receptionist: // r WHAT'S your <u>NAME</u> //

We might paraphrase this: 'I have a name here for two o'clock: is it yours?' With proclaiming tone, the same elicitation might well be taken as a denial that the patient *did* have an appointment: 'There is no entry in my book for two o'clock: tell me who you are so that I can look for your name elsewhere'. Alternatively, the receptionist might be asking for the patient's name before consulting the book, so that he/she knows what to look for, but this would be, from our point of view, a crucially different situation: the receptionist would be working with no basis on which to make a provisional assumption. For another example, we will take:

(212) // r WHERE does <u>THIS</u> train go to please //

Here, the passenger would usually be checking whether this was the train he/she wanted to catch, and referring tone would therefore be expected. Exceptionally, we might hear a proclaimed version, with a predictably different effect. Having asked several times and on several platforms and been told that it is *not* the train he/she wants, our passenger might ask,

(213) // p and WHERE does <u>THIS</u> train go to //

the implied absence of prediction in his/her enquiry signalling exasperation: 'as far as *he/she* can see from the way the system seems to be working, it could be going anywhere!'

The general truth that underlies examples like these is that the distinctions realised by choices in the P/R system cut right across the traditional, grammar-based classification into yes/no and information types. With both types, the choice of a referring tone projects the speaker's wish to have his/her assumptions confirmed with respect to a truth which he/she presents as having been negotiated. Proclaiming tones used with both types project a wish that the respondent should provide a selection from a so-far unnegotiated set. Note that if we have a set of discourse conditions which motivate proclaiming tone in a yes/no elicitation, there is always a related information elicitation that could be used with proclaiming tone. If a speaker asks

(214) // p IS it an <u>EL</u>ephant //

as a guess, he/she confesses to the same state of ignorance as he/she would confess to by saying

(215)   // p WHAT IS it //

but a change of tone, to

(216)   // r WHAT IS it //

would result in a different state of speaker/hearer convergence being projected. Similarly, if an information elicitation with a referring tone is motivated, so is a yes/no elicitation with a referring tone. By asking

(217)   // r WHAT TIME is it //

a speaker displays the same kind of anticipation of the response as he/she would by asking:

(218)   // r IS it FIVE yet //

The frequently-heard assertion that *wh-* interrogatives have some natural affinity with falling intonation can probably be attributed to a cause similar to that which we suggested lies behind the association of polar interrogatives with rising intonation: requests for information of, for instance, the *how, where* or *when* kind may well occur most frequently in situations where the information is so far unnegotiated. But, again, we have to recognise that such a tendency – if, indeed it exists – is a fact about situations and not a deterministic relationship between 'question type' and tone selection.

A rough, working characterisation of the significance of either kind of elicitation with referring tone might be 'I think I know the answer; please tell me whether I am right'. For either elicitation with proclaiming tone, we might propose 'I don't know the answer: please tell me'. We must not, however, interpret 'knowing' too literally here, particularly as many questions seem to have a predominantly social motivation.

Social elicitation

We have so far taken it for granted that elicitations serve to remove uncertainty in the mind of the speaker: he/she seeks to have his/her world view modified by the hearer, or to have confirmation that his/her present world view coincides with that of the hearer. In reality, many real-life elicitations – among them the most common – have the pursuit of world-view convergence as only a very minor part of their purpose.

Questions of the 'How are you?', 'Did you enjoy the play?' kind, which Malinowski described as 'phatic', are seldom asked for the sake of eliciting information of any kind. Question and answer procedures – enquiries about people's well-being, friendly instructions couched in the grammar of questions like 'Won't you sit down?' – all these play such an important part in social intercourse that it would be surprising if the generalised social implications of tone choice were not often found to be predominant. All our comments on elicitations above can be interpreted in a way which makes direct reference to the social conditions of separateness and togetherness: 'This I ask as *I*, having a so-far different view of the world from the one I assume you have', or 'This I ask as one who presumes that *our* world views are assimilated'. It is consistent with all we have said so far that an intended social effect should provide the primary motivation for an elicitation when the value participants are likely to place upon the exchange of information is minimal. Phatic questions have some kind of social bridge-building as their aim; it is therefore to be expected that they will customarily have a referring tone, the tone choice that insinuates togetherness:

(219) // r HOW ARE you //

(220) // r DID you have a good HOLiday //

If otherwise similar items have proclaiming tones, they are usually not heard as phatic at all. For instance,

(221) // p HOW ARE you //

sounds like a doctor's question, a genuinely interested enquiry about how effective the last prescription has been. It is well known that people are usually expected to reply in the affirmative to questions like (220). The speaker behaves as if *yes* were already negotiated and the respondent is normally willing to conform. If we discount the content of the exchange, as we can with real phatic events, we can say that the speaker projects a state of generalised social convergence and the respondent acquiesces in it. This is so far a ritualised procedure that the truth of the response is scarcely a consideration. It is slightly less obvious how such convergence can be achieved with elicitations like:

(222) // r HAVE you had a long JOURney //

Here, the speaker adopts the tone appropriate to a situation in which he/she has already formed an idea of what the response will be. The respondent, for his/her part, might find it less easy to be untruthful about the length of his/her journey than the state of his/her health. Conveniently, however, the form of the enquiry does not reveal what the enquirer's expectations are: either *yes* or *no* could be regarded as confirming the undeclared – and in all probability non-existent – assumption. Behaving as if one had a hunch by no means depends upon one's actually having one.

Although we may surmise that the primary intention of an utterance like (222) will often be the establishment of a comfortable social relationship, the enquirer does actually end up being better informed. Such a mixture of informational and social effects attaches to most elicitations outside the fairly clearly-defined set of conventional phatic enquiries. In order to demonstrate how this mix can interact with some of the other variables in a context of interaction, we will consider some of the possible local interpretations of the following items with a referring tone:

(223)   // r are YOU mister <u>SMITH</u> //

(224)   // r WHAT'S your <u>NAME</u> //

(i)   We have already seen that either of these might serve to check a supposition about the identity of the person addressed. In some situation where such checking was essential for the proper conduct of business – in ensuring, for instance, that a patient saw the right dentist – the passage of information could be said to be the primary motive.

(ii)   Elsewhere, the same utterance might be said to be socially including in its principal intent. In an encounter at a party or at the beginning of an interview, where names were in reality already known or else of little real consequence, the most noticeable effect of the tone choice might be to bring a newcomer into a working relationship with an already established group.

(iii)   Either elicitation may be anticipatory. By insinuating that he/she only needs to have his/her assumptions confirmed, the speaker can make use of a conversational ploy similar to 'Am I right in thinking that you are . . . ?' Clearly, 'Are you the person I believe/hope/expect you are?' is a more promising opening to a social encounter than 'I don't know you from Adam: who are you?' which might, under some circumstances, be a rough interpretation of either of our examples if they had a proclaiming tone.

(iv) Either may be preparatory. Checking that one has the right person is usually a precursor to telling them something: 'Are you Mr Robinson? . . . I have a message for you'; 'Is that John over there? . . . I must go and have a word with him'. So strong is the presumption that people do not usually initiate this kind of world-matching procedure *unless* they intend to go on and say something that is potentially world-changing for the hearer, that the latter might find it rather puzzling if the interlocutor did not go on. This seems to apply to purely phatic exchanges just as much as to those that serve a necessary purpose of ensuring that background assumptions are correct before business is embarked upon. Notice that (166) // r is THIS the SHEFfield train // exemplifies the preparatory function in a special way: there may be no further verbal business except a polite acknowledgment, but it would be odd if the enquirer got the expected affirmative response and then made no move to get on the train.

In trying to disentangle some of the strands of significance a single combination of referring tone and question might have, we are not, of course, suggesting that (i)–(iv) are to be thought of as separate 'functions' of intonation. We should probably feel that several, if not all, those effects could be attributed in some measure to most occurrences of items like those cited. In this connection, as elsewhere, it is all too easy to become pre-occupied with the multiplicity of possible local meanings and lose sight of what they all owe to the general values that accrue to selections in the P/R system.

7

The pitch sequence

In Chapter 3 we emphasised the importance of separating out the distinctive contributions that key and termination make to the communicative value of the tonic segment. There were, however, some choices in both these systems whose significance we did not cover there. In order to accommodate these in our descriptive system, we shall now consider how the two independently-meaningful variables work together to build up a unit of greater extent than the tone unit, an entity to which we shall give the name pitch sequence*.

When we discussed the syntagmatic relationships that give internal cohesion to tonic segments in Chapter 2, we stopped short of asking whether any kind of syntagmatic patterning might be found to cover longer stretches of speech. The tacit assumption has been, so far, that the stream of speech can be adequately represented as a chain of tone units, placed end to end as it were, with speaker-options associated with each link in the chain. What we now wish to show is that sequences of tone units contract syntagmatic relations with each other, in such a way that certain speaker-choices affect the communicative value of the sequence rather than that of any of its constituent tone units. In doing so, we are borrowing the concept of a hierarchy from grammar. Just as the grammarian seeks to associate different systems with units like word, group, clause and sentence, so we shall extend our conceptual apparatus to allow for choices associated with the pitch sequence as well as those we have already associated with the syllable and the tonic segment.

Low termination

A conspicuous omission from Chapter 3 was any discussion of the communicative value of low termination. The reason for this is that proper explication requires reference to the pitch sequence. Indeed, we can most convincingly introduce the latter by now making good the omission.

It will be recalled that we generalised the values of high and mid termination by saying that they projected an expectation of a certain kind of reaction from the hearer, a reaction which, in certain circumstances had the audible realisations, adjudicating *yes* and concurring *yes*, respectively. We shall now say that low termination projects *no expectation* of a comparable kind. A set of examples will serve to enlarge on this statement:

(225)   // p ARE you <u>SURE</u> // p that THAT'S the so^{LUTion} //

(226)   // p ARE you <u>SURE</u> // p that THAT'S the so<u>LUT</u>ion //

(227)   // p ARE you <u>SURE</u> // p that THAT'S the so_{LUTion} //

Example (225) is a request for a decision: 'Are you, or are you not, sure?'; (226) invites concurrence: 'Will you confirm that you are sure?' A projection common to these two is the expectation that the other party will make an immediate response addressed to the polarity element of the question. We cannot claim that addressees will necessarily say *yes* or *no* in reply to either: he/she may prevaricate, satisfying the expectation of pitch concord with a dummy *well*, perhaps; or he/she may assert dominance by declining to match key to termination at all. What we can say is that whatever he/she does will be heard in the light of the quite specific expectation the question sets up. The conditions projected by (225) and (226) are those in which, in common parlance, it might be proper to speak of the respondent giving (or failing to give) a straight answer to a straight question.

Both of these examples are invented ones. The third of the set was actually heard in a broadcast discussion. Its context was as follows:

(228)   Chair: // p ARE you <u>SURE</u> // p that THAT'S the so_{LUTion} //

Discussant: // r ^{MOST} of the folk i've _{TALKED} to // r a<u>BOUT</u> the provision // p seem FAIRLY con<u>CERNED</u> // about . . .

Transcribed fragmentally like this, the second speaker's contribution promises to be a *non-sequitur*; as it develops, however, it turns out to be a comment highly relevant to the question of the rightness or otherwise of the visualised 'solution'. What he/she does is to interpret the chair's utterance as a signal to open a discussion: the latter is understood to have set up the question as something to be debated rather than as a proposition whose truth is to be immediately adjudicated upon or concurred with; under these circumstances a response 'Yes, I am' with either adjudicating or concurring force would be considered grossly inadequate. The significance of the low termination in the question is clear; it is an essential part of the 'free hand' that the chair gives to the discussant to tackle the topic in whatever way he/she chooses that there are no projected constraints to begin in any particular key.

By using a yes/no question for exemplification, we are able to say that there is no immediate expectation of concurrence or adjudication. To generalise to all possible cases, we have to remember that the 'active' responses expected by high termination and the 'passive' responses expected by mid termination do not always lend themselves to such easy conceptualisation. We have to be content with the formal statement: low termination projects no expectation that the response will begin with a particular key choice. The significance of this freedom has to be approached by examining the local effect in particular cases.

In (228) the respondent exercises the 'freedom' by selecting high key; but examples can be found of both mid-key and low-key openings. What is absent from these moments of speaker change is the kind of locking of utterance to utterance that pitch concord results in (or the conspic-uous absence of such locking if the second speaker declines to follow suit). We can summarise the range of possibilities we have described as follows:

high termination ⸺ expects ⸺ high key
mid termination ⸺ expects ⸺ mid key

low termination ⸺ permits choice of ⸺ high key
⸺ mid key
⸺ low key

There is a suggestive similarity between the effect of the low-termination choice and the end-points of other units that the analyst sets up to deal with different aspects of linguistic patterning. Most obviously, the end of the grammatical sentence is the point at which all the constraints inherent in its own organisation cease to be effective: when a new sentence begins, the speaker or writer has freedom to do as he/she pleases in so far as the making of grammatical choices is concerned. Recent work in discourse analysis suggests also that in the unit 'ex-change' certain limitations upon what the parties to an interaction may do remain operative just so long as the exchange lasts. By saying now that low termination is the realisation of pitch-sequence closure we are recognising that here, too, the unit ends when the constraints that derive from a particular kind of language organisation are reduced to zero. The pitch sequence is that stretch of discourse within which each speaker's actual behaviour can be judged against the expectation of utterance-to-utterance locking. More simply, the pitch sequence is defined as a stretch of speech which ends with low termination and has no occurrences of low termination within it.

We are not, of course, suggesting that pitch sequences are necessarily coterminous with sentences or exchanges. If they were, this area of phonology would add nothing to what could be said about the utterance in grammatical and discourse terms. The constraints are of quite different kinds; for instance grammatical constraints limit the speaker's freedom in formulating his/her own utterance, while those associated with termination affect the freedom of the other party. The method we have to follow is to think in terms of points of maximum relaxation in the three distinct organising procedures and to note what the effects are when they do, and when they do not, co-occur.

Internal and external choices

At this point it is helpful to abandon, for the moment, the preoccupation with communicative value that we have tried to maintain throughout the book, and focus instead upon the phonetic realisations of key and termination – pitch level. Common sense, and rudimentary physiological considerations, might lead us to expect a progressive fall in pitch over a considerable stretch of speech. This expectation would be satisfied either by a gradual fall or by a stepping down from high key to low termination, as in:

(229) $//\,p$ so ^{HOW} $\underline{DID}$ $//\,p$ the ACcident $_{\underline{HAP}pen}$ $//$

We might say that this pattern was a simple reflex of the operation of the breathing mechanism.

There are, in fact, few occasions, in real discourse, when this simple pattern is followed. It is instructive to consider, one by one, the various factors that cause it to be modified.

(i) If, as we have said, pitch-sequence closure is communicatively significant, the descent to low termination will not be mechanically determined, but will be the result of the speaker's choice. In consequence, the length of pitch sequences, as measured in tone units, is extremely variable. An intentional deferment of closure and our physiologically-based expectation would both be satisfied if an indefinite number of mid-key/mid-termination tone units intervened between the first and last:

(230) $||$ p so ^{WHAT} WERE $||$ p the REST of you DOing $||$ ... $||$ p when the ACcident $_{HAP}$pened $^{||}$

(ii) A minor complication is the fact that in every minimal tonic segment key choice and termination choice are interdependent. A minimal tonic segment in a tone unit that is initial or medial in the pitch sequence does not materially upset the pattern:

(231) $||$ p so $\underline{\frac{HOW}{}}$ $||$ p did the ACcident $_{HAP}$pen $^{||}$

(232) $||$ p so ^{WHAT} WERE $||$ p you DOing $||$ p when the ACcident HAPpened $^{||}$

In an example like the following, however

(233) $||$ p so ^{HOW} DID $||$ p it HAPpen $||$

the goal of low termination can be reached only by the addition of a 'dummy' tone unit:

(234) $||$ p so ^{HOW} DID $||$ p it HAPPen $||$ p in $_{FACT}$ $^{||}$

(iii) More worthy of note, we saw in Chapter 3 that the speaker does *not* have to follow the steady downward movement that physiological considerations alone would lead us to expect. It is only if all intermediate tone units are presented as additive (mid key) and as pre-empting concurrence (mid termination) that we shall get sequences with this simple shape. All the instances of high and low key that we discussed in Chapter 3, as well as the instances of high termination, can be looked upon as departures from it:

(235) $||$ r ap$\underline{\frac{PARently}{}}$ $||$ p he GAMbled $||$ p and $\underline{\frac{LOST}{}}$ $||$ ...

(236) $||$ r ap<u>PARently</u> $|| p$ he <u>GAM</u>bled $|| p$ and $\underset{LOST}{}$ a <u>FOR</u>tune $||$...

(237) $||$ r ap<u>PARently</u> $|| p$ he <u>GAM</u>bled $|| p$ and LOST a <u>FOR</u>tune $||$...

After any 'high' choice, the downward stepping movement is resumed, unless and until the speaker makes another 'high' choice. Example (236) shows that choice of low key to indicate equative value does not necessarily involve choice of low termination, and hence pitch-sequence closure, unless there is a minimal tonic segment, as in:

(238) $||$ r ap<u>PARently</u> $|| p$ he <u>GAM</u>bled $|| p$ and $\underset{\underline{LOST}}{}$ $||$...

We shall refer to all these diversions from the high-mid ... mid-low route as internal choices* of key and termination (that is to say, internal to the pitch sequence) to distinguish them from the low termination choice, which as we have said is always sequence-closing, and the key choice that comes immediately after it in connected discourse, that is to say the sequence-initial key choice.

The key choice at the beginning of the pitch sequence

We demonstrated the existence of a three-way choice of key at the beginning of the pitch sequence by examining an example in which the pitch-sequence closure coincided with a change of speaker. It is easier to approach the communicative value of the choice if we take one in which the same speaker continues after the sequence boundary, as happens in:

(239) $|| r^{\text{I think on the}}$ <u>WHOLE</u> $|| r+$ that THESE of<u>FIC</u>ials $|| p$ do a reMARKably good $\underset{\underline{JOB}}{}$ $|| r$ we $^{\text{HAVE to re}}$ <u>MEM</u>ber $|| r$ that they're re<u>QUIRED</u> $||$...

The value of the high-key choice realised in *have* can best be conceptualised if we refer to the comparable grammatical unit, the sentence. Standard orthographic practice recognises that contiguous sentences can contract three different kinds of relationship with each other, relationships that are indicated by the use of the semi-colon, the colon and the full stop. The rules that govern the use of these conventions are notoriously difficult to formulate and it is easy to point to inconsistencies between how writers actually punctuate and how contiguous pitch sequences are related. We could plausibly speculate that punctuation practices are based on an incomplete apprehension of how pitch sequences relate to each other in the spoken language, but to do this would be to go beyond the legitimate business of this book. All we shall do is to compare the two sets of relationships in an informal way in the hope of clarifying the set that are realised intonationally.

If we take the full stop as the marker of maximal disjunction between sentences, we can say that a high initial key choice separates off pitch sequences in a similar way. In (239), once the speaker has said that the officials do a remarkably good job, he/she proceeds to make another observation whose relevance to the previous one may not necessarily become apparent for some time. Although all the sentences in a paragraph can be shown to be related to each other in many different ways, those that are separated by full stops have a greater measure of independence from their neighbours than those that are separated by other means.

At the other end of the scale, we may compare sentences separated by a colon with pitch sequences where the second of a pair has low initial key. Many uses of the colon can be explained in terms of existential equivalence between the relevant items: it is not infrequently possible to substitute a phrase like '. . . that is to say . . .' (as this sentence demonstrates). A low-key sequence opening articulates a similar relationship between sequences, as for instance in:

(240) $// r^{\text{I think on the}}$ WHOLE $// r+$ that THESE of FICials $// p$ do a

reMARKably good $_{\text{JOB}}$ $// p_{\text{i}}$ THINK they're ter$\underline{\text{RIF}}$ic $//$

Two points arise from a consideration of this example. The first is that the existential equivalence implied is a relationship between the first pitch sequence *considered as a whole*, and the second *considered as whole*. If the second continues

(241) $// p^{\text{i}}_{\text{THINK}}$ they're ter$\underline{\text{RIF}}$ic $// p$ they hardly EVer make a

$^{\text{mis}}_{\text{TAKE}}$ $//$

it is the whole of this stretch that is presented as an existentially valid reformulation of the preceding three tone units. The distinction between inter-sequential relationships and meaning increments which attach only to a single tone unit is essentially what separates sequence-initial from internal key choices. The second point is that, although a step up to mid termination in an example like (241) opens up the possibility of indefinite extension of the new pitch sequence, sequences having initial low key tend to be short, often amounting to no more than one tone unit in length:

(242) $\parallel p^{\,i}$ THINK they're terRIFic $\parallel$

Just as the tone unit may be realised by a single syllable, so a pitch sequence may be realised by a single tone unit: a low-key/low-termination *yes* may be simultaneously described as a pitch sequence, a tone unit and a syllable.

Of the three comparisons, that between the semi-colon and the sequence-initial mid-key choice is perhaps the least satisfactory. The relationship we wish to propose for both is something that is neither maximally disjunctive nor fully equative. The term 'additive' that we introduced earlier to characterise internal mid key will serve our turn here, with certain adjustments. Consider:

(243) $\parallel r^{\,I}$ think on the WHOLE $\parallel r+$ that THESE ofFICials $\parallel p$ do a reMARKably good $_{\text{JOB}}$ $\parallel r+$ they're ALways poLITE $\parallel r$ they work inCREDibly long HOURS $\parallel p$ and they hardly EVer turn anyone ^{a}WAY $\parallel$

Here, the second pitch sequence goes well beyond giving an existential paraphrase of the first. We can nevertheless hear it as in some sense enlarging upon the assertion that is made therein: rather than breaking new ground, the speaker presents a kind of re-analysis of what he/she has just said. We have to distinguish between this function of 'adding to' the precision of the preceding pitch sequence, and the functions we have associated with the other two key choices: of leaving the assertion behind, as it were, and going on to make another one; or of simply reformulating it. There is probably no point in our description where the need to see the value of three terms in the system as mutually defining is greater than it is here. If, for the sake of restricting our technical terminology, we employ the labels contrastive, additive* and equative for inter-sequential relationships as well as for the values that accrue to internal key choices, we have to beware of the need not to read an overprecise notional interpretation into them.

Again, we should note that the additive relationship, like the equative relationship, holds between the whole of the one pitch sequence and the whole of the next. It is worth dwelling briefly upon this fact and upon its implications for a model of the real-time generation of speech. It means that in both cases, the speakers have to be thought of as in some way restricted in what they do in the second pitch sequence by what they have already done in the first. Without pressing the parallel too far, we can usefully import such concepts as 'subordination' or 'binding' from grammar. This then provides us with another way of characterising the 'contrastive' inter-sequential relationship realised by high key. Since the new sequence is a new start, there are no such constraints upon what the speaker can do. It also makes clear why there is little point in talking of a relationship between 'whole sequences' in the case of the high-key choice: it is, perhaps, less misleading to say that the latter signals an *absence* of relationship (in a strictly limited sense of 'relationship'), and to acknowledge that the temporal extent of elements that are 'not related' is not an issue.

In order to illustrate the effect of the three-way choice, we have invented examples in which there seems to be a peculiar appropriacy between the key choice and the lexico-grammatical composition of the second pitch sequence. This is to say, we have followed our practice of suggesting contexts of interaction in which the key choice is effectively redundant. It is necessary, once again, to correct the impression that may be given by this technique that the key choice is determined by other features of the utterance. It would, in fact, be possible to invent contexts of interaction in which any one of the second pitch sequences we have used for exemplification could be presented as being related equatively, additively or not at all to the preceding one. All our examples have done is to try to exploit the probability of particular intonational and lexico-grammatical couplings. To demonstrate the autonomy of the intonation choice, we will consider another example, one which we will first give in standard orthography:

> 'The child lives in a somewhat narrow world of personal contacts. Things hardly come within his experience unless they touch, intimately and obviously, his own experience, or that of his family and friends.'

We will assume – what is demonstrably the case – that most people asked to read these two sentences aloud assign a pitch-sequence boundary to the sentence boundary. Having done this, they then have the choice of beginning the next sequence with either high, mid, or low key:

$$
(244) \quad \ldots // \text{ of PERsonal } \underline{\text{CON}}\text{tacts} // \quad \begin{array}{l} \text{high} \ldots \\ \text{mid} \ldots \\ \text{low} \ldots \end{array}
$$

It will be seen that the content of the two sentences is such that the second could be regarded as a reformulation of the first, as an amplification of it, or as a new, 'unrelated' assertion – as a movement away from speaking of the significance of people to speaking of the significance of 'things'. When presented as a pair of sentences like this, any one of the three readings would be justified. In the context of a real, situated discussion of educational matters, it is possible, but not certain, that the context of interaction would indicate a preference for a particular one.

The significance of the pitch-sequence closure: 1

The argument presented in the last section depends upon a prior assumption that one sequence has ended and another is about to begin. Having said something about inter-sequential relationships, we now have to enquire into the significance of pitch-sequence closure. What motivates the speaker's decision to close it at one point rather than at another? Or, given our definition of the pitch sequence in terms of the occurrence of low termination, what is the 'considerable stretch of speech' we referred to earlier that the speaker separates off as having its own particular kind of internal relationships and as contracting other kinds of relationship with entities similarly separated off? We have mentioned the fact that pitch sequences resemble sentences and exchanges in that they exhibit a kind of running down of the constraints that unify them. Indeed, we made this observation our reason for associating sequence closure with low termination and thus for representing the pitch sequence in the terms we have just set out. There are problems as yet unsolved in separating out the specific contributions that the three kinds of boundary make to the communicative value of the utterance. The kind of generality of description that we have sought in attributing value to other intonation features could probably be achieved only in the context of a fully worked-out model of discourse which relates the three modes of organisation, grammar, discourse and intonation, in some explicit way. Needless to say, such a model is not yet available, and even if it were, it is unlikely that an account of it could be accommodated here. The most we can do is to illustrate some of the local effects of non-congruency between the pitch sequence and each of the other kinds of unit.

Taking the grammatical unit first, we will consider two different situations:

(i) The sentence extends over more than one pitch sequence:

Sentence	
Pitch sequence	Pitch sequence

(ii) The pitch sequence extends over more than one sentence:

Pitch sequence	
Sentence	Sentence

An example of (i) is:

(245) $|| p$ ^{IF you'd} <u>KNOWN</u> $|| p$ it was WORTH so _{MUCH} $|| p$ WOULD you have _{PARTed with it} $||$

To interpret this, we might say that the speaker sets up a hypothesis which he/she asks the addressee to consider before answering. There is very little difference between (245) and

(246) $|| p$ sup^{POSE you'd} <u>KNOWN</u> $|| p$ it was WORTH so _{MUCH} $||$ p WOULD you have _{PARTed with it} $||$

except that the latter has a sentence boundary as well as a pitch-sequence boundary. In both cases, the message seems to be something like 'consider first, and then answer'. At this point we can usefully refer to a distinction that would usually be regarded as being inherent in the grammar of a pair of sentences. We should usually say that

'Go out. Close the door behind you.'

requires two responses, while

'When you go out, close the door behind you.'

requires only one. We are here thinking of 'responses' as observable physical activities, but we can easily extend the use of the word to include the 'considering' and 'answering' that we have said are the consecutive expectations of (245). If we think, in an informal way, of continuous discourse looking for a series of discrete reactions using 'discrete' in the sense that 'considering' and 'answering' might be said to be discrete reactions to either (245) or (246), then what our examination of (245) suggests is that the pitch-sequence boundary contributes significantly to our apprehension of how many reactions are expected.

One reason why we cannot here pursue the question of how grammar and intonation interact in realising this aspect of discourse structuring is that the sentence-like objects that constitute much spontaneous speech differ from the sentences the grammarian describes. The independent structuring function of the intonation is perhaps most obvious in an utterance with anomalous grammar:

(247) $// p ^{THAT}$ PICture $// p$ we SAW in the $_{GALLery} // p$ WHAT did

you $_{THINK}$ of it $//$

Again, the hearer is invited first to recall, then to comment on the picture; we can compare the effects with those of 'What did you think of the picture we saw in the gallery?'

We can illustrate the situation we designated (ii) with a pair of sentences which, because they fall within a single pitch sequence, can be thought of as representing a single assertion for the hearer to react to:

(248) $// p$ i ^{SAW} PETer $// p$ he was CHANGing his $_{LIBrary book} //$

This can be paraphrased in either of two ways: 'Because Peter was changing his library book, I saw him'; or 'I know Peter was changing his library book because I saw him'. Whichever of these is appropriate, it brings out the unitary nature of the communication and distinguishes it from:

(249) $// p$ i SAW $_{PETer} // p$ he was CHANGing his $_{LIBrary book} //$

In his last version, the two assertions are presented as discrete items, to be apprehended, and possibly to be reacted to, in turn. The pattern is to be expected where two pieces of information would almost certainly count as unrelated assertions:

(250) $//p$ i SAW $_{\underline{PETer}}$ $//p$ he's BOUGHT a new $_{\underline{CAR}}//$

We can connect the fact that there seems to be no way of recasting the two sentences as a single one without altering their implications with the probability that this item would not occur in a version like (248).

The significance of pitch-sequence closure: 2

Another way of showing how one's sense of the discreteness of the pitch sequence impinges upon one's general apprehension of the communicative value of utterances is to examine a third type of proclaimed *yes* that may follow an utterance by another speaker. It is exemplified in:

(251) Speaker A: $//p$ can you TELL me your ad$\underline{DRESS}$ please $//$
       Speaker B: $//p$ NUMber $\underline{FIVE}$ $//p$ the $\underline{AV}$enue $//$
       Speaker A: $//p_{\underline{YES}}//$

It is evident that neither an adjudicating *yes* nor a concurring *yes* would be appropriate in the kind of situation where this type of question is normally asked. We can take it that Speaker A is bound by normal conversational practice to accept that what B has said *is* the case: in other words that *yes* does not represent a sense selection. Its production is therefore to be accounted for in terms of the intonation choice associated with it: it serves to close the pitch sequence. The effects of such closure are best appreciated by comparing (251) with an example in which Speaker A goes straight on to ask another question:

(252) Speaker A: $//p$ can you TELL me your ad$\underline{DRESS}$ please $//$
       Speaker B: $//p$ NUMber $\underline{FIVE}$ $//p$ the $\underline{AV}$enue $//$
       Speaker A: $//r$ is THAT be$\underline{YOND}$ the traffic lights $//$
       Speaker B: $//p \underline{YES}//$
       Speaker A: $//p_{\underline{YES}}//$

Here, the sequence-closing *yes* is withheld until after B's second response. The effect is to unite the contents of the two responses into a piece of information that is in some sense unified, so that A reacts to it as a whole. We may say that what he/she wants to know is where B lives, and he/she finds it necessary to ask two questions to find out. The effect is different if he/she closes the pitch sequence before asking the second question:

(253) Speaker A: // p can you TELL me your adDRESS please //
       Speaker B: // p NUMber FIVE // p the AVenue //
       Speaker A: // p $_{YES}$ // r is THAT beYOND the traffic lights // . . .

Here, he/she reacts to one piece of information and then, by opening a new sequence with mid key, goes on to elicit another piece that he/she expects to be an enlargement of the first.

When discussing elicitations in Chapter 6, we found it necessary to distinguish between utterances that were represented as having world-changing implications for the hearer and utterances whose end was to obtain another utterance which would have world-changing implications for the speaker. We can now see that a speaker can impose a unity upon a number of items of news, whether he/she or his/her hearer is the putative beneficiary. Just as he/she can invite a single reaction to a number of assertions by including them in a single pitch sequence, so he/she can signal his own acceptance of a number of responses as if they were one piece of news by manipulating the pitch-sequence boundary.

Evidently, this kind of comparatively long-term organising of the conversation constitutes the kind of 'control' that we have associated with dominant speakers. We can, in fact, say that pitch-sequence closing, like selection of the + versions of referring and proclaiming tones, is the prerogative of the dominant participant. While teachers and doctors characteristically mark the fact that one – possibly complex – piece of information has been satisfactorily elicited by closing the sequence, it is scarcely within the competence of pupils and patients to do so. A low-termination *yes* interpolated into informal conversation is fairly easily recognisable as a bid to assume dominance. In all these cases, the speaker who ends the ongoing sequence indicates his/her intention of continuing in, or taking over, dominant speaker role.

In each of our examples Speaker A does, in fact, exert dominance in two ways when he/she produces the low-key *yes*. He/She closes the pitch sequence and, in doing so, he/she disregards the expectation of pitch concord set up by B's response. Under certain circumstances, we might imagine B availing himself/herself of one of these options without having to do the other:

(254) Speaker A: // p can you TELL me your ad<u>DRESS</u> please //
       Speaker B: // p NUMber <u>FIVE</u> // p EASTern _{<u>AV</u>enue} //

B's temporary assumption of dominance here can be seen in the fact that he/she restricts the options available to A. Since the pitch sequence is now closed, the latter has no choice but to accept the content of the response as a discrete piece of information and, if he/she wants enlargement, to open a new sequence. Often responses like that in (254) have local implications of the '. . . and that's all I'm going to tell you!' kind: a child who responded as in (255) might well be accused of being sulky:

(255) Adult: // p WHY haven't you eaten your <u>PUD</u>ding //
       Child: // p i DON'T _{<u>LIKE</u> it} //

8

Orientation

By making a choice in any of the intonation systems we have so far described, a speaker makes some kind of assumption about what he/she takes, for present purposes, to be the state of understanding between him/her and a hearer. We have said that all the choices are of the either/ or kind, and that whatever decision he/she makes with respect to any one of them has implications for the context of interaction he/she projects. We must now consider another possibility, namely that some stretches of language are presented in such a way that their projections are neutral with respect to one or more of those features of a context of interaction that intonation realises.

Tone choice

A convenient way into the matter is to consider the case of someone reading aloud. When faced with a printed item to read, let us say with

> 'Mary was a teacher'

the reader may approach the task in either of two ways. He/She may, in the terms we have used to describe a communicative event, assume some particular context of interaction and make tone choices accordingly. Any such hypothetical discourse setting would, of course, involve assumptions that would affect all the intonation choices in the ways we have now indicated, so that the resulting phonological shape of the reading might be any one of a considerable number of possibilities. For the moment, we will consider only those decisions that affect the choice between proclaiming and referring tone, and say that among the patterns our reader might choose are:

(256) $// r \underline{\text{MAR}} \text{y} // p$ was a $\underline{\text{TEACH}}\text{er} //$ and

(257) $// p \underline{\text{MAR}} \text{y} // r$ was a $\underline{\text{TEACH}}\text{er} //$

An alternative course would be to interpret the request to read the item out simply as an invitation to say what was printed on the paper. In this latter event, there would be no grounds – not even hypothetical grounds – for making choices in the P/R system, because whatever discourse conditions applied to the composition of the original sentence, if indeed there ever were any, would be irrelevant to the task that was presently in hand. We could expect the whole sentence to be proclaimed as

(258) // p MARy was a TEACHer //

but what was now proclaimed would be information about what was printed, not information about other aspects of the speaker/hearer worlds. The speaker would not be asserting 'who was a teacher' nor 'what Mary did for a living', but *what the printed item said*. We must be clear that the significance of proclaiming tone in (258) is quite different from what it would be in an otherwise similar tonic segment in:

(259) // r at THAT time // p MARy was a TEACHer //

A way of capturing the difference might be to say that the use of quotation marks, thus,

'Mary was a teacher',

would have an appropriacy for (258) that it would lack for (259) – unless, of course, the speaker were quoting someone else's assertion about Mary's job.

To deal with the phenomenon, we shall make a distinction between direct orientation* and oblique orientation*. By the former we shall mean the kind of set towards an identified hearer that results in choices meshing with some putative state of convergence. By the latter, we shall mean a set towards the language item which results in its being presented as a specimen of the language. In the latter case, the speaker does not presume that the linguistic sample he/she reads out has any kind of communicative significance in anyone's world, except as an uninterpreted entity. It may help to characterise the result if we remember that he/she does not take any responsibility for the truth of any assertion he/she may make: he/she can read out our sample in full knowledge that Mary practises medicine and not be guilty of lying.

Neither does he/she accept responsibility for its intelligibility or grammaticality: it is no concern of his/hers whether it is a 'good' linguistic sample.

To avoid misunderstanding, it should be made clear that when people read aloud it is far more usual for them to adopt a direct, listener-sensitive stance, interpreting the text as if they were themselves the originator of whatever message they assume it embodies. The efficacy of all the examples we have used so far in this book depends, in fact, on the ability of readers to read these aloud as though they were acts of communication performed in the situations we have specified for them. We can, nevertheless, make a conceptual separation between an activity called 'reading out' and a different activity called 'reading aloud' in which the reader makes contextual projections. Provided this separation is clear, some acts of reading provide apt illustrations of oblique orientation.

Consider now an oblique reading of a longer piece of text. It would be consistent with all we have so far said for a sentence, selected arbitrarily from an earlier paragraph in this chapter, to be read as a string of proclaimed tone units. The following will probably be recognised as one variant form of the activity of reading out:

(260) // p to DEAL with this phe<u>NOM</u>enon // p we shall MAKE a dis<u>TINC</u>tion // p between diRECT orien<u>TA</u>tion // p and oBLIQUE orien<u>TA</u>tion //

(that is what this sample of language, regarded as a linear string of components, says).

An alternative, and one which readers of this book may find more closely resembles their own practice and observations, has a 'level' tone (symbol o) in place of some of the proclaiming tones:

(261) // o to DEAL with this phe<u>NOM</u>enon // p we shall MAKE a dis<u>TINC</u>tion // o between diRECT orien<u>TA</u>tion // p and oBLIQUE orien<u>TA</u>tion //

'Level' tone is the one we have not yet encountered. Its presence marks its tone unit as part of oblique orientation. It can now be related to the other tones by representing the decisions the speaker has to make for each tone unit as follows:

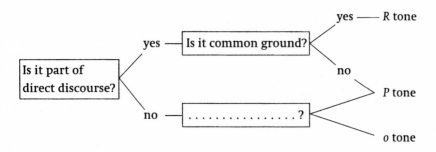

Two facts are made apparent by this diagram. The first is that P tone plays an equivocal role in two different systems: it occurs in tonic segments which contain information that is presented as world-changing for the hearer; and it occurs in obliquely-oriented parts of an utterance that report 'this (linguistic item) is what is written here'. The other fact is that we have not yet established the basis on which the decision as between P tone and o tone is made in oblique discourse. What question should occupy the empty box?

If we look at example (261) from the point of view of someone processing a randomly-chosen sentence from left to right, the first point at which any grammatically permissible sentence could end is after *distinction*. After that, since a distinction must necessarily be made between two things, the next feasible end-point is after the second occurrence of *orientation*. The intonation treatment we have proposed is related to these observations: 'level' tones occur when tone unit boundaries do not fall at points of potential completion, 'falling' tones occur when they do. We can take this as a first approximation to what happens when samples of language are presented obliquely. In so far as it is a satisfactory approximation, we can see that the decisions are made on the basis of the speaker's apprehension of the linguistic organisation of the item, not on any assumptions about how the utterance meshes with a context of interaction. This much is to be expected from our characterisation of oblique orientation as a set towards the language sample: syntactic completeness is an attribute of the sample and is in no way dependent on the here-and-now state of speaker/hearer convergence. We cannot claim, however, that it is any more than an approximation. The circumstances in which oblique presentation takes place, whether it is manifested as an act of 'reading' out or as some other activity, and also the different apprehensions among speakers and readers of where potential completeness is to be found, result in a good deal of irregularity in performance. We might, for instance, think that awareness that the item cannot end after *phenomenon* depends upon a more superficial engagement with the material being read than does the awareness that it cannot end after the first *orientation*. It is a matter of observation, not only that different speakers assign *P* tones and *o* tones differently at many points in the same text, but also that a particular speaker does so differently on first and subsequent readings. If we keep in mind, however, that decisions as to completeness are made by speakers in real time and on the basis of the limited evidence that an oblique engagement with the quoted item makes available, we can complete the diagram as follows:

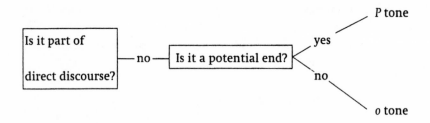

Ritual as oblique orientation

The features we have attended to in 'reading out' as a manifestation of oblique discourse belong also to various kinds of speech activity that we can group together informally under the heading 'precoded'. If we reflect upon the different things a speaker may do, there is an easy conceptual transition from articulating what it (that is to say, the written text) *says*, to repeating what they (that is to say, people in general) *say*, and to what is (customarily) *said*. Certain language formulae which accompany oft-repeated business are frequently spoken in a way which absolves the speaker from any responsibility for here-and-now appropriateness to a changing state of convergence. The implication can be said to be something like: 'These are not my words addressed particularly to you on this occasion; they are rather a routine performance whose appropriateness to our present situation we both recognise'. Perhaps the most obvious exemplification is the parade-ground command:

(262) // 0 STAND <u>AT</u> // . . . // p <u>EASE</u> //

We need not dwell upon the fact that this is unmistakably *not* a newly-minted locution, shaped by the speaker with the unique moment of utterance in mind. The 'zero' tone, followed by the exaggerated pause, typifies almost to the point of caricature the exploitation of a suspension effect that derives from the 'incompleteness' meaning we referred to in the last section. It is interesting, too, that the speaker usually assumes a special voice quality for the event. Distinctive stylistic features like this are often associated with oblique discourse, a fact which we can readily connect with what we have said about the peculiar discourse conditions: orientation towards the linguistic item as some kind of pre-determined script or text that has to be performed is more likely to result in the observance of a vocal stereotype. We should expect that in direct discourse variations in pause length and in voice quality would show the same kind of sensitivity to the changing – and comparatively unpredictable – speaker/hearer relationship as tone choice shows. Stereotyping, if it occurs in such discourse, is usually heard as impersonation of a third party.

Another kind of event often characterised by oblique orientation and having its own accompanying set of stylised vocal features is the public recitation of prayers and other liturgical material:

(263) // 0 alMIGHTY <u>GOD</u> // 0 <u>FOUN</u>tain of all <u>GOOD</u>ness // 0 we HUMbly be<u>SEECH</u> thee // . . .

No doubt the special need for speakers who recite corporately to keep together contributes to the characteristic style here. But it is not without interest that the oblique mode, as it is exemplified in much ecclesiastical practice, fits the assumptions that underlie the act of prayer much more satisfactorily than those we have ascribed to direct discourse. The concept of a unique conversational nexus, with its associated notions of shared and separate worlds, creates obvious problems when related to the act of speaking before an omniscient deity. The properties of generality and distancing which all ritual uses of language probably share, attach in some sense to both the discourse types we have mentioned, though they would usually be held to serve very different ends.

High stylisation is not a necessary concomitant of oblique orientation.

In almost any verbal business which repeats established and frequently-rehearsed procedures we can expect to find instances of it surrounded by direct discourse and often distinguished from the latter by nothing more than the use of level tone. We will take a single discourse type, classroom interaction, as a source of a few illustrations.

The string of directives like

(264)   // o STOP <u>WRIT</u>ing // o PUT your pens <u>DOWN</u> // o LOOK this
        <u>WAY</u> // . . .

which, with minor variations, is a recurrent feature of a large number of lessons, qualifies for oblique orientation as semi-ritualised practice. By adopting an oblique stance, the teacher separates off some part of the management of the class from the here-and-now negotiation of common ground that most of the lesson consists of: for the moment, teacher and class are in the world of time-honoured and well-understood procedures.

Elsewhere in a lesson, oblique orientation may serve to mark off a piece of received wisdom, or – more accurately – its traditional verbal embodiment, which encapsulates the results of some kind of exploratory, interactive teaching. When, for instance, having demonstrated some of the mathematical properties of the triangle, a teacher turns away from the class and declares

(265)   // o <u>SO</u> // o the SQUARE on the hy<u>POT</u>enuse // o of a RIGHT
        angled <u>TRI</u>angle // o is equal to the SUM of the <u>SQUARES</u> // p on
        the OTHer two <u>SIDES</u> //

he/she can be said to be invoking the definitive expression of a truth that the class and the teacher have just been demonstrating to each other. We might say that by this act he/she lifts the whole business out of the area which, up to now, has been assumed to be negotiable, and gives it the status of immutable knowledge.

Another frequent occasion for oblique orientation is the kind of 'template' technique teachers use for eliciting contributions from students, a technique that is exploited particularly, but not exclusively, in language lessons:

(266)   Teacher: // o he BOUGHT it <u>ON</u> // –
        Pupil: // p <u>THURS</u>day //
        Teacher: // p he BOUGHT it on <u>THURS</u>day // p <u>YES</u> //

(267) Teacher: // o the LONGest side IS // . . .
     Pupil: // p the hyPOTenuse //
     Teacher: // p GOOD //

In language lessons, most of the material is introduced as samples of the target language rather than as contributing to an ongoing discussion for which a context of interaction exists. In (266) 'He bought it on Thursday', regarded as nothing more than a sentence, represents a selection and combination of elements which the teacher assumes can be assembled on the basis of whatever input has just been provided. By following level tone with a silence he/she is conventionally understood to be asking someone to complete the linguistic specimen. (267) is similar. It presupposes that the sentence, 'The longest side is the hypotenuse' is implicitly available in the context, so that its constituents can be jointly put together by teacher and pupil. This kind of co-operative recital of a received formula differs markedly from the process of negotiation that direct orientation involves.

Orientation and verbal planning

We have said that the existence, on paper or in the speaker's memory, of a pre-coded or partially coded formula is one condition that favours a set towards the linguistic organisation of the utterance rather than towards the hearer. Another, quite different, condition can be the fact that encoding has not yet been achieved and is presenting some difficulty for the speaker. Psycholinguistic studies have pointed out interesting relationships between 'hesitation phenomena' and the cognitive activity that verbal planning entails. Both 'pauses' and 'pause fillers' have been found to have significance in this connection. The implications of such studies fall outside the scope of this book. We should note, however, the tendency already referred to for pauses to follow instances of level tone. To this we can add the observation that pause-fillers, themselves non-selective items (since they have no word status within the language system) frequently serve as dummy carriers of the tone:

(268) // o he SEEMS rather A-A-A // . . . p AGitated // r to ME //

(269) // r and the ANswer // o is ERM // p TWENty //

Alternatively, the level tone may be realised in a conventional word:

(270) // o he SEEMS RAther // ... p AGitated // r to ME //

(271) // r and the ANswer // o IS // ... p TWENty //

In the four examples we have devised, it will be seen that the 'level' tones occur in the immediate neighbourhood of tone choices that indicate direct orientation. They can be taken as representative of a very common kind of orientation change at a point where the speaker has momentary coding problems – difficulty, perhaps in finding the words he/she wants or in marshalling the information he/she wants to present. The occurrence of such changes in spontaneous speech accounts, in large measure, for the fact that transcripts of naturally occurring discourse are often less 'tidy' than those we have used to illustrate our exposition. Without pursuing the matter further, we can say that, in a general way, the more a speaker is 'thinking on his/her feet' the more common they are.

Temporary preoccupation with some problem of message organisation is, then, another cause of the speaker switching from the more 'normal' concern with meshing an utterance with a putative state of convergence, and focusing instead on the linguistic properties of the utterance itself. Among the various manifestations of oblique discourse, it is possible to make a distinction between those where the mode is sustained for a comparatively long stretch of speech (as, for instance, a prayer), and those like the occurrences of 'level' tone in the neighbourhood of a hesitation, which tend to be single tone units interpolated into direct discourse. It is worth noting that there is no formal difference between the latter kind of involuntary, on-line orientation change and certain occurrences of 'level' tone-plus-pause which we must assume are introduced deliberately for rhetorical effect. When a teacher says

(272) // r the WORD for RUBbing // o IS // ... // p FRICtion //

it is unlikely that he/she is actually needing time to think of the word he/she wants to introduce, but by acting as though this were the case he/she makes the class wait for it, presumably with the intention of increasing its impact when it comes.

The difficulty of recognising the results of orientation change

It would be misleading to suggest that it was always easy – or even possible – to recognise a stretch of oblique discourse in any particular piece of data. Even if we take an occurrence of 'level' tone as an unequivocal marker of an oblique stance, we are still left with the fact that 'falling' tones have a double function. This problem of interpreting transcriptions, however, does no more than reflect what common sense says is true of a great deal of spoken discourse: people manifestly *do* include in utterances that are predominantly now-coding and pragmatically organised, chunks of language that are presented simply *as* chunks of language. The re-use of well-established verbal formulae, self-quotation, and remembered runs of particular phrases, all feature extensively in some types of discourse, and probably to some extent in most. We cannot expect any descriptive system to resolve ambiguities that inhere in the data. Its function is rather to show how such ambiguity can arise: if an account of intonation did not show how it was possible for an uncommitted recital of a ready-made formula to be mistaken for a committed and hearer-sensitive assertion, we might feel that it was missing out on an essential feature of that state of interpenetration of speaker's and hearer's worlds on which the whole of the present description has been based.

Two points are, perhaps, worth underlining. One is that if choices in the P/R system are indeed related to the speaker's apprehension of that state of interpenetration, it is inconceivable that the system should provide him/her with no means of uttering linguistic items aloud without having to commit himself/herself to such an apprehension: an escape route is an essential requirement in any system of the kind we have postulated. The other point is that overt markers of orientation change are just as much formal features as are all the other intonational categories, and are thus available for exploitation. To describe an oblique stance as resulting from a disengagement from any sort of context of interaction is by no means to say that 'level' tone may not be adopted *as if* such disengagement had taken place for any number of different local purposes.

The most important reason for recognising the direct/oblique distinction is not the extent to which it has to be taken into account in interpreting most kinds of data, so much as the confusion that failure to do so creates when we try to understand and give formal expression to the system. Over and above this theoretical concern, brief mention of two practical matters will not be out of place here. The first is very much to the present point. No written presentation of a description of intonation can be successful unless readers can reproduce the illustrative examples in a particular way: and any written item can be read out obliquely. Sooner or later, the user of such a description – including this one – has to come to an awareness of the difference between the two modes and so to resist the temptation – even at third, fourth and fifth readings – to 'hear' them as no more than linguistic specimens. The second, related, point concerns intonation in second-language classrooms, the setting in which it has probably attracted more attention than in any other. The teaching of languages unavoidably depends largely upon the presentation of specimens: teachers provide, and students repeat, specimen words, specimen phrases and specimen sentences. It is easy to recognise the intonation of oblique orientation in much of the language that results; and because there is usually comparatively little language that is directed by a speaker to a hearer in situations where it is the existential sense that has communicative value, this mode provides the most frequent model for the learner. Pedagogical as well as other considerations make it essential to take note of how hearer-sensitive intonation choices differ from those motivated by a limited engagement with the language item.

Prominence

We have said (Chapter 2) that prominent syllables, like tones, are distributed on the basis of what context of interaction the speaker chooses to project. We must ask now on what basis these are distributed when the speaker is not involved in an interaction which would give reasons for assigning them to certain places rather than others.

We noted in Chapter 2 that the citation forms of some words have the two-prominence pattern of the extended tone group

(273)   // CON des<u>CEND</u>ing // ; // UN<u>NAT</u>ural //

a treatment which distinguishes them from the occurrence of the same items in context, when a single prominence is normally sufficient to signal the intended sense selection:

(274)   // a CONdescending <u>MAN</u>ner //

(275)   // his MANner was condes<u>CEND</u>ing //

(276)   // it was UNnatural be<u>HAV</u>iour //

(277) // his beHAViour was un<u>NAT</u>ural //

We can find a precise replication of the two patterns in forms like

(278) // r well <u>I</u> think // p he was condes<u>CEND</u>ing //

(279) // r well the WORD <u>I</u> should use for him // p is CONdes<u>CEND</u>ing //

in which the second can be heard as a kind of word quotation that would usually be represented in writing as 'condescending'. The quotation marks alone sometimes serve to indicate that a word is being quoted as, for instance, in: 'They accused him of behaving in a "condescending" manner', and this practice, too, has an intonational parallel in

(280) // r they ac<u>CUS</u>ED him of be<u>HAV</u>ing // p in a
CONdes<u>CEND</u>ing // p <u>MAN</u>ner //

an utterance which differs in its implications from:

(281) // r they ac<u>CUS</u>ED him of be<u>HAV</u>ing // p in a CONdescending
<u>MAN</u>ner //

On the strength of examples like these, we might propose a general-isation which would be captured by:

(282) // it's un<u>NAT</u>ural // (That is the *sense* I select)

(283) // it's UN<u>NAT</u>ural // (That is the *word* I use)

There are several reasons, however, why such a generalisation can be no more than tentative. One is that local interpretation cannot always be reinterpreted so as to give satisfying support to this view of the formal opposition. Many hearers report that the effect of the additional promi-nent syllable in items like (283) is to give 'emphasis' to *unnatural*. Emphasis is an ill-defined property that can accrue to any number of the phonological choices this book has described when they occur in certain situations, and what the hearers may be reacting to is the effect of deliberate, careful choice of an expressive word as an alternative to merely using the word that comes to mind immediately as a convenient realisation of the intended sense. Another problem is that it is not always easy to separate out double prominences that might be serving to realise word quotation from cases where it provides opportunity for additional choices in one of the other systems, as for instance in

(284) $//\ p$ but it's $UN_{\underline{NAT}ural}\ //$

where the combination of mid key and low termination can only be
achieved if there is prominence in *un-*.

More seriously, however, there are many occasions when the choice
between 'This is the sense I select' and 'This is the word I use' has no
noticeable repercussion in the containing discourse: when the two
activities must be judged as, for all practical purposes, amounting to the
same thing. It is therefore impossible to conceptualise the consequences
of substituting the alternative choice, and therefore to test the validity of
the generalisation in any but a small number of cases. Moreover, the
phonological distinction in question applies only to those words whose
citation forms happen to have two prominent syllables. In

(285) $//$ it's $\underline{NAT}ural\ //$

the observable consequences of sense selection and word quotation are
identical.

None of this amounts to a retraction. There is strong, if only
intermittent, reason for supposing the generalisation we proposed is
substantially correct. What is evident once more, however, is that in
seeking the consequences of a switch in orientation we encounter a great
deal of uncertainty. And we can attribute this once more to the general
operation of the intonation system we have described, and to general
considerations we can feel confident in applying to the production of
spoken language. The peculiar relationship between language as sample
and language as situated communicative event has necessarily to be
taken into account, even if its details cannot always be established.

The same applies if we now take one further step in the examination
of prominence distribution. The distinction that was exemplified by the
two treatments of *unnatural* can be shown to operate in phrases. In

(286) $//\ r$ the HOUSE on the $\underline{COR}ner$ is $//\ p$ for $\underline{SALE}\ //$

non-prominent *for* reflects the absence of sense selection at this point. If
prominence is assigned, as in

(287) $//\ r$ the HOUSE on the $\underline{COR}ner$ is $//\ p$ FOR $\underline{SALE}\ //$

we seem to have a quotation of the message in the sign outside the house. Similarly, the second of the following differs from the first in that it makes use of a (quoted) technical phrase:

(288) // r the DISpute // p was SETtled out of COURT //

(289) // r the DISpute was SETtled // p OUT of COURT //

It seems to be commonly the case that, if a word is self-evidently not selective in the context of interaction but is nevertheless made prominent, this can be taken as an indication that the speaker is temporarily withdrawing from involvement in the convergence process: that is to say he/she is adopting an oblique stance. Compare:

Speaker A: Why hasn't John finished his project?

(290) Speaker B: // p he HASn't been very WELL //

(291) Speaker B: // p he HASn't BEEN very WELL //

(292) Speaker B: // p he HASn't BEEN VERy WELL //

While (290) provides a directly-oriented response to the enquiry, the additional prominences in (291) and (292) make it clear, to different degrees, perhaps, that Speaker B takes no responsibility for the assertion: the response is merely a disengaged quotation of what has been said to be the reason.

Examples like these last two provide us with a way of accounting for at least some of the cases where tone units have more than the expected two prominent syllables. There is a readily recognisable relationship between the written and spoken forms of the following:

(293) Autumn is a 'season of mists and mellow fruitfulness'.
       // r AUtumn // p is a SEASon of MISTS and MELlow
       FRUITfulness //

(294) The jury consisted of 'twelve good men and true'.
       // r the JURy conSISTed // p of TWELVE GOOD MEN and
       TRUE //

Or we may compare the conversational style of

(295) // r HE who HESitates // p is LOST //

(296) // r you can TAKE a horse to WATer // p but you CAN'T make it
       DRINK //

with the non-interactive quoting of a selection of English proverbs:

(297) // p HE who HESitates is <u>LOST</u> //

(298) // p you can TAKE a HORSE to WAter but you CAN'T MAKE it <u>DRINK</u> //

What principles underlie the distribution of prominent syllables in such cases as these? Since there is no apprehension of a context of interaction to guide the decisions, we may surmise that they are assigned in a more-or-less automatic way to the open-class words. In so far as the open/closed distinction can be taken to be part of the speaker's linguistic knowledge, it provides a communicatively neutral distribution that presupposes engagement with nothing more than the language system – a condition we have associated with oblique orientation.

Yet again, the tentative nature of all this has to be stressed. When we examine the small number of tonic segments having more than two prominent syllables in naturally-occurring speech, we cannot usually associate them with transparently recognisable acts of quotation of the foregoing kind. More often we have to recognise that something like the distancing effect of quotation might be a factor in the context of interaction as the analyst can reconstruct it. There is no place where access to the participants' minds would be more desirable, nor where the illusion that it can be achieved more dangerous. The fact that such tone units *are* so infrequent, and seem in some sense to go against the 'normal' propensities of interactants lends strong support to the view that they, on the one hand, and the one or two prominence types on the other constitute a formal choice of central significance. Starting with the well-attested phenomenon of word citation, and applying the logic of the descriptive system we have set up, we can go some significant way towards demonstrating that the opposition between them is related to the choice of orientation.

9

Retrospect

The possibility of there being multiple prominent syllables in a tonic segment was only one of the ways in which we anticipated that applying the categories set up in Chapter 1 might be less than entirely straightforward. Those categories were, as we said, presented in advance of an exploration of the meaning system on which their justification depended. Now that we have discussed each of the separate meaning contrasts in turn, we are in a better position to consider the other problems we expected. This, together with a number of other tidying-up operations that require reference to the entire meaning system, makes up the substance of the present chapter.

Incomplete tone units

When examining spontaneously produced speech of any considerable quantity, we are likely to find stretches, bounded by pauses, which do not have the constituency structure we have described and attached meaning to. To deal with such cases, first recall that level tone often precedes a pause, introduced either for thought or for effect:

(299) // o THEN THE // . . . // p SYStem was changed //

Tonic segments like // o THEN THE // satisfy the requirements of our description in that they have the essential element, a tonic syllable. In so far as they arise from a real need for planning time and are not theatrically contrived to keep the hearer waiting, we can regard their occurrence as a direct consequence of the fact that speech is created in real time. A similar cause seems to lie behind the occurrence of two kinds of truncated tone unit, that is to say kinds of tone unit that lack a tonic syllable:

(300) // he WAITed - // p he THOUGHT he'd better WAIT //

(301) $||$ and – $||$ p he THOUGHT he'd better <u>WAIT</u> $||$

These examples are similar to each other in that the speaker breaks off the first tone unit before he has reached the tonic syllable, a fact that is shown in the transcription by the absence of a tone symbol and underlining. They differ from (299) in that there is no level tone, so that – in the terms we used in the last chapter – there is no reason for saying that a switch to oblique orientation accompanies the hesitation: we might, perhaps, speculate that whatever planning, or replanning, activity the speaker engages in does not involve him/her in temporary disengagement from the interactive relationship in the way that instances of (299) do. Our two examples differ from each other in that the speaker of (301) does not get as far as producing a prominent syllable, while the speaker of (300) does. As the prominent syllable is the place where key is selected, only the former type occurs as re-selection in the key system:

(302) $||$ p he <u>GAM</u>bled $||$ and LOST – $||$ p and $_{LOST\ a}$ <u>FOR</u>tune $||$

Here, the speaker can be thought of as in some sense 'remembering' that the hearer will regard the two assertions as existentially equivalent and as revising the projected assumptions accordingly. The example can be compared with (300), where the self-correction seems to have to do with the precise verbal formulation of the assertion.

It will be appreciated that this view of things arises directly from the decision to treat the 'breaking off point' and associated pause as criterial for transcription purposes: pauses are always treated as tone unit boundaries. The decision to do the transcription in this way is, of course, a purely descriptive one. Instead of regarding the *and* in (301) for instance, as a 'failed' tone unit, it would have been possible to transcribe the whole item as:

   $||$ p and—he THOUGHT he'd better <u>WAIT</u> $||$

It will be evident that in speaking of planning procedure, self-correction, and such matters we are glancing at psycholinguistic and perhaps neurolinguistic questions which lie outside the scope of this book and which, in any case, are only poorly understood at the present time. It seems proper to regard truncated units as manifestations, not of the working of the meaning system we set out to describe, but of the speaker's moment-by-moment difficulties in employing it. We adopt the transcription conventions exemplified by (300) and (301) simply to have a consistent way of dealing with pauses, a way which, because it is as arbitrary as we can make it, avoids prejudging anything that further systematic study of their psycholinguistic significance might reveal.

'Phonetically continuous' pairs of tone units

If the tone unit boundaries are conventionally recognised at all pauses, it is not necessarily the case that there is anything we could describe as a pause between contiguous tone units. A third matter we avoided facing in Chapter 1 was the possibility of there being no phonetic reason for recognising a boundary between stretches of language that have separate tonic syllables and are therefore, in our account, to be regarded as separate tone units. We spoke of the enclitic segment of one tone unit merging into the proclitic segment of the next, so there was no perceptible point at which one ended and the next began. Some phonologists have treated such a stretch as a 'bi-nuclear' tone unit, and the easiest way to take up the matter here is to consider an utterance of the kind that has been said to exemplify the phenomenon:

(303)   She's a clever girl is Mary

The improvised notation is intended to represent a 'fall' in *girl* which is phonetically continuous with a 'low rise' in *Mar-* (cf. Halliday's (1967) 'one-three' pattern). What we have to do is to justify treating this as

$$// p \text{ she's a CLEVer } \underline{\text{GIRL}} // r^+ \text{is } \underline{\text{MAR}} \text{y} //$$

or, if we adopt the convention, allowed for on page 14, of leaving out the boundary symbol when there is no phonetic reason for using one, as:

$$// p \, r^+ \text{she's a CLEVer } \underline{\text{GIRL}} \text{ is } \underline{\text{MAR}} \text{y} //$$

Compare first the meanings of (303) and an otherwise similar example in which the elements occur in reversed order:

$$// r^+ \text{AS for } \underline{\text{MAR}} \text{y} // p \text{ she's a CLEVer } \underline{\text{GIRL}} //$$

In both cases, 'She's a clever girl' is proclaimed as a truth that the speaker regards it as necessary to recognise. The fact that *girl* is prominent (though obviously not a sense selection) carries a special implication: the appellation 'clever girl' is applied in much the same way as 'honourable man' is applied to Brutus. When 'As for Mary' comes first, it may well constitute a sense selection; the similar 'is Mary', coming after the assertion, probably does not. The prominent syllable can therefore be taken to be there in order to carry intonational meaning. Specifically, the referring tone introduces an assumption of mutuality: the speaker expects the hearer to go along with him/her in his/her recognition of Mary's cleverness. A similar example with mid key would invite concurrence ('She is, indeed'). With low termination it has implications of finality, and it is very likely to be exchange-closing:

> A: What a marvellous performance!
> B: She's a clever girl, is Mary.

The dominant version probably reinforces the sense that this is the end of the matter, but notice that a non-dominant version

$$// r \text{ is } \underline{\text{MAR}} y //$$

is also available. Finally, it is worth pointing out that the perception of 'phonetic continuity' usually depends upon there being only one prominent syllable in the second tone group. The following exploits the same set of choices as (303):

(304) $// p$ she's a CLEVer $\underline{\text{GIRL}} // r+ \text{ is } _{\text{MARy}} \underline{\text{ROB}} \text{inson} //$

The linear extent of the tone unit

One reason why the question of whether examples like (304) ought to be analysed as 'bi-nuclear' tone units or as concatenations of two separate tone units has been seen as a crucial one is that in some descriptions the way a stretch of speech is divided into tone units is assumed to be meaningful in itself. A common procedure has been to postulate a normal or 'unmarked' coincidence of the tone unit with a grammatical unit – usually the sentence or the clause – and discuss intonational meaning in terms of possible departures from this norm. We have so far considered the significance of the division of an utterance into tone units only by implication. Most obviously, it can be seen as a reflex of the speaker making successively different choices in one or more of the systems: tone, key and termination. Each time, he/she makes a new choice he/she needs a new tone unit to make it in. So, the fact that

(305) // r MAR y // p was a TEACHer //

has two tone units and not any other number is the result of *Mary* and *teacher* being assigned different values with respect to the P/R opposition. Having said this, we have exhausted the significance of the division. In addition, the limitation on the number of prominent syllables in a direct-mode tone unit would seem to account for:

(306) // p he TRIED HARD // p to MASter it //

Here, all the intonation choices in the second tone unit simply replicate those in the first. Much data provides us also with examples of a third kind:

(307) // p he WAITed // p to HELP her //

Here, neither the need for re-selection nor the need to avoid more than two prominent syllables can be advanced as the reason for the division. We must take it that when there is a simple choice between presenting matter as a single, unified, sense selection, as in

(308) // p he WAITed to HELP her //

and presenting it as two consecutive sense selections, as in (307), the difference has to be accounted for in some way; and accounting for it requires that something is added to what has been said so far. All three of these kinds of situation will be kept in mind in what follows.

The question that inevitably suggests itself at this point concerns the relationship of intonational segmentation to grammatical constituents. The principle insisted upon at the beginning of this book was that the formal oppositions that constitute the intonation system should be kept quite separate in the description from formal oppositions of other kinds. If we begin with the tone unit boundary that results from the making of a new choice in one of the intonation systems, it is easy to show that there is then no deterministic relationship between the two modes of organisation. The following set of examples shows how any grammatical constituent can be singled out and given proclaiming value while nothing else in the utterance is proclaimed:

(309) // p PETer // r SENT the letter to MARy //

(310) // r PETer // p SENT // r the LETter to MARy //

(311) // r PETer SENT // p the LETter // r to MARy //

(312) // r PETer sent the LETter // p TO // r MARy //

(313) // r PETer sent the LETter to // p MARy //

It is not easy to contrive sentences which yield a set of equally plausible versions when an utterance is dealt with in this way, even when some adjustments are made to the distribution of prominent syllables. Indeed, readers may have difficulty in imagining likely contexts for some of the versions offered. It is important, though, to stress that what one is involved in *is* the finding of appropriate contexts and not distinguishing between utterances that are well-formed and deviant. The relevant features of a context of interaction which would match any of the variants can be arrived at by considering the projections made by the intonation. If, for instance, (312) is adjudged less probable than some, it is because we are required to envisage a situation in which *to* (existentially selected, perhaps, from a set like *to/about/for*) can properly be presented as the only world-changing element in the sentence.

In the foregoing paragraph, we have confined our attention to choices in the P/R system. It would be possible to show that any constituent could carry a differential choice in any of the systems: any word could, for instance, be the domain of a contrastive high-key choice. Examples occur in naturally-occurring speech, moreover, in which tone units coincide with stretches of speech that grammarians would not describe as constituents at all:

(314) // p but PETer always DID // r preFER BRITish cars //

(315) // p i LIKE it in SPITE of // r+ its WEAKness //

To investigate the third kind of situation, where neither constraint upon the number of prominent syllables nor the need to make a new choice provides a motive for segmentation, we will examine the following pairs of examples:

(316) // p he reTURNED HAP py //

(317) // p he SEEMED HAP py //

(318) *||p* he WAITed to HELP her *||*

(319) *||p* he WANTED to HELP her *||*

(320) *||p* he PUT it on the SHELF *||*

(321) *||p* he FOUND it on the SHELF *||*

(322) *||p* he was EATing a SANDwich *||*

(323) *||p* he was BUYing a SANDwich *||*

For the first member of each of these pairs, it would be fairly natural to substitute a version having two tone units with identical choices in all three systems, as for instance:

(324) *||p* he reTURNED *||p* HAPpy *||*

A similar substitution for the second member of each pair would produce a rather strange-sounding utterance. These observations can be connected with standard punctuation conventions. Each of the first members have commonly occurring alternative forms:

He returned happy.   He returned, happy.
He waited to help her.   He waited, to help her.
He found it on the shelf.   He found it, on the shelf.
He was eating a sandwich.   He was eating – a sandwich.

Such alternatives are scarcely available for second members: 'He seemed, happy', and so on, would probably be said to be incorrectly punctuated.

Note first that, punctuation conventions notwithstanding, division into two tone units sounds natural enough in examples like the second ones when one of the other reasons exists for making the division:

(325) *||r* he SEEMED *||p* HAPpy *||*

(326) *||p* he REALly SEEMED *||p* HAPpy *||*

Our examples would seem, then, to provide us with the basis for enquiring into what constrains division when neither of these reasons does exist.

Each pair is, of course, capable of differentiation on syntactic grounds, as are the 'divided' and 'undivided' versions of the first members. At first sight it is tempting to seek a grammatical explanation of the matter in spite of earlier denials that this is proper procedure. Note, however, that such an approach would assume a quite different explanation in each case. Whatever syntactic analysis was used, it would contrast the members of each pair in different ways, and would moreover assign a new syntactic difference to the large number of other pairs that might be used to illustrate the same general point. This would not, in itself, be an objection; but it turns out that a consideration of what they all have in common leads to a very much simpler explanation.

To follow this line of enquiry, we have to remind ourselves once again of the real-time, linear aspect of the presentation and decoding of speech. It would not be difficult to imagine a speaker articulating

(327)   // p he reTURNED //

and then adding – quite literally as an afterthought –

(328)   // p HAP py //

It would be harder to imagine anyone launching on

(329)   // p he SEEMED //

before he/she had in some sense 'planned' the whole utterance 'He seemed happy'. What distinguishes all our first pair-members from our second is the likelihood of their being the outcome of such piecemeal assembly and presentation. What the second members have in common is a much reduced likelihood that the speaker will prepare and present his/her message in this kind of incremental fashion.

Again, we must make clear that the description of the intonation system stops short of making any statements of a specifically psycholinguistic or neurolinguistic nature. The simplistic and pre-theoretical account of one aspect of the process of speech production is offered only as a means of giving greater conceptual substance to the notions we introduced under the heading of 'selection' in Chapter 1, and to which we have subsequently made constant reference. In saying that there is no obvious problem in the way of a speaker saying // p he FOUND it // and then, after an interval, of adding // p on the SHELF // , we are saying, in effect, that *found* and *shelf* are two separate independent selections in two separate sense paradigms, and informally attributing some kind of psychological reality to the fact:

How did he get it?

He	found	it on the	shelf
	bought		market stall

In saying that 'He put it on the shelf' is not easy to treat like this, we are saying that *put it on the shelf* would usually be presented as a unified sense selection:

What did he do with it?

He	put it on the shelf
	sold it
	gave it to his younger brother

We must be clear, too, that everything said above has to be couched in terms of probability. We cannot say that the forms we have described as unlikely will never be produced under the pressures that involved, real-time conversational conditions can generate.

As for the other situation, that exemplified by (326), in which the absence of a division would result in a tonic segment having more than two prominent syllables, it is tempting to speculate that this might reflect some constraint inherent in whatever mechanisms are involved in the production and reception of speech. All that can be done within the present frame of reference is to report the normal upper limit of two as an empirical fact.

Redundancy

There is one further question that was discussed at some length in Chapter 1 and that we can now usefully return to in the light of subsequent chapters. This is the quite different matter of the phonetic realisation of the meaningful categories. Several reasons were advanced for avoiding an inappropriate preoccupation with the phonetic fact: for seeking first to establish the formal oppositions even if this meant being rather vague about how the physical realisations were to be recognised. We argued that language users must be presumed to operate within an area of tolerance where intonation is concerned not dissimilar to that which enables them to recognise substantially different segments as variants of the same phoneme. It can now be suggested that the nature of the meaning system provides yet another reason for expecting that there will be problems in framing precise realisation statements which relate intonational meanings to objectively describable physical events.

As was said at the outset, this description was arrived at by a process which involved, among other things, listening to, and evolving transcription conventions for, a considerable amount of recorded data. Many of the people who have already made use of it in connection with their own research programmes have been similarly occupied. Most report – and in doing so confirm the author's experience – that there are occasions when it is just not possible to make a confident decision with regard to a particular choice in one of the systems on acoustic grounds. It is, perhaps, worth stressing that in saying this one is making an observation about the data and not about the applicability of any particular set of descriptive categories: a pitch movement which was heard uncertainly as either a 'rise' or a 'fall-rise' would stand in the way of producing a definitive and replicable transcription whatever categories were used.

Undoubtedly, the conditions under which most naturally occurring data have to be recorded cause some of the difficulties. Recording facilities are an invaluable – probably indispensable – aid in this kind of enterprise, making it possible to listen to the same sample over and over again; but if we are to escape from the limitations of real-time transcription, we have to accept limitations of other kinds. These include the effects of background noise, the siting of microphones relative to speakers, and the unsatisfactory acoustic properties of most places where spontaneous verbal interaction takes place. Even when data is collected under carefully controlled studio conditions it sometimes seems that the processes of recording and reproduction introduce distortions that can affect the hearer's certainty about what he/she is hearing. And it seems to be the case, too, that most transcribing decisions that are problematical remain so when we have recourse to instrumental analysis. It is not, however, any of these potential hindrances to the production of a perfect transcript that we have now to focus upon. These might all be said to be the result of extraneous interference coming between the speaker and the analyst. Additionally, we need to take account of another obstacle that is directly attributable to the speaker's output. To appreciate the reasons for its existence, we shall reconsider both the general nature of the meanings conveyed and the general nature of their phonetic realisation.

We have remarked several times upon the need for stating the communicative value of intonation in terms of the *projected* contextual implications of the tone unit: only if we regard intonation as a 'situation-creating' device, rather than as a means of relating the utterance to some pre-existent situation, can we give proper recognition to its ability to carry independent meanings. We have said that to do otherwise would be wrongly to represent intonation as a set of variables whose deployment we could predict if we had adequate knowledge of the ready-made situation. To say all this is not to deny, however, that the projections will normally be those which the speaker assumes will be acceptable to his/her hearer; nor is it to deny that for much of the time in many conversations what is projected will do no more than mesh with a context of interaction that is fully and unequivocally appreciated by both parties. To put the matter another way, understanding the value of intonation as a potentially independent carrier of meaning requires that we attend specially to those instances in which it is not situationally redundant; understanding just how a speaker operates the system in a physical sense may require that we give some attention to those instances in which it is.

The effects of the kind of redundancy we mean can be readily appreciated if we look for a moment at an example in segmental phonology. Consider the question/answer pair:

Q: What does John think about it?
A: John doesn't know yet.

It is highly likely that a speaker who substitutes /don/ for /dʒon/ in the response will be 'heard' as saying /dʒon/. Because of the clear expectations set up in the question, the phonetic feature which distinguishes a careful pronunciation of *John* from a similar pronunciation of *Don* is not significant. Only in a situation where John and Don were two people and both potential candidates for mention would phonetic explicitness be an important consideration. Conditions somewhat similarly apply to the likely intonation treatment of the name in the response:

(330)   // p john doesn't <u>KNOW</u> yet //

From the first speaker's point of view, the situation is one in which the non-selective value of *John* is certain. It follows that he/she will be strongly pre-disposed to hear it as non-prominent whether the acoustic features which would mark it as unambiguously non-prominent are present or not. And what applies to the prominence/non-prominence distinction applies also to all others in the intonation system. Each one articulates an assumption about an aspect of speaker/hearer understanding. Often the assumption is found upon what to the hearer must be self-evident and readily recoverable circumstance. To the extent that this is the case, the acoustic properties of the speaker's utterance will be easily anticipated.

Being frequently redundant in a communicative situation is by no means a special characteristic of intonation. There is, however, something about the nature of the phonetic variables concerned that should encourage us to take special note of it. Pitch, loudness and time are all continuously variable attributes of the speech signal. The operation of each of the intonation systems depends upon our identifying either/or choices on the basis of evidence which can only be described acoustically in terms of continuous variation. Some implications of these facts can be appreciated if we return to the comments we made on the relative pitch treatment of two syllables on page 1:

```
              ┌  S2 (high)
              │
S1 ······     ┤  S2 (mid)
              │
              └  S2 (low)
```

Provided we keep in mind all that has been said about likely concomitant variations on other parameters and about not being dogmatic about the treatment of any one syllable in isolation (see pp. 2–6) we can now interpret this diagram as representing the pitch levels associated with two consecutive key choices. It will be recalled that we said the crucial matter was the pitch level at S2 relative to that at S1. We said also that when there was a difference between levels, the extent of the difference was not a consideration in determining what formal choice had been made. It will be seen that, since no meaningful difference need be more than what is perceptible, the ease with which differences will be recognised must be expected to vary from time to time. There will, in fact, be no identifiable point at which the phonetic difference between a high and a mid choice, or between a mid and a low one will 'disappear':

```
          ┌  S2 ──────────┐
          │                │
S1 ───────┤  S2 ──────────┼─→──
          │                │
          └  S2 ──────────┘
```

Considerations like these apply to all the acoustic variables that enter into the realisation of all the intonation categories. It would require a lengthy, and inappropriate, digression to make a comparison with that which applies to word-defining segments. It is enough to recognise that intonationally-significant differences are subject to a much simpler process of 'expansion' and 'compression' than they are.

Taking into account the two factors we have discussed, it seems not improbable that the phonetic realisation of intonation will alternately fade and re-assert itself according to whether the associated communicative value can be assumed to be predictable by the hearer or not. In saying this, we are speculating that economy of physical effort is one of the factors that governs a speaker's behaviour. There is little in the way of firm evidence to support such an argument, so that it has to rest largely on appeals to inherent probability and common observation. Nevertheless, the argument can scarcely be ignored, for it has important implications. The status of a set of descriptive categories, and the problem of applying them in the analysis of data, have to be viewed quite separately. The kind of evidence that does lend some kind of support to this position is of the following kind. In some kinds of discourse, like that produced in classrooms, most intonation choices are fairly clearly distinguishable, presenting few problems for the transcriber: the tendency seems to be towards high acoustic definition rather than otherwise. In other discourse, like much desultory conversation, the reverse is the case. We can associate this with the fact that the teacher is setting up a framework of understanding which is very largely of his/her making, and appreciates the need to exaggerate the distinctions upon which its successful communication depends. The working understanding that underlies much informal conversation is such that the speaker may assume that he/she does not need to make sharply-defined differences to ensure that his/her communicative intent is appreciated.

Clearly, if there were a large number of cases where the transcriber was unable to make a decision, this would throw doubt upon the validity of the whole description. The working basis for the latter has been, as it has to be, a firm centre comprising the majority of unproblematical speaker-choices, from which extrapolation can plausibly be made to the rest.

Some further examples to illustrate the use of the various speaker-options

Prominence

(331) // it's a <u>BLACK</u>bird //

(332) // it's a BLACK <u>BIRD</u> //

The treatment of well-known pairs like this conforms to the pattern we have described. In (331), *blackbird* is presented as a single sense selection in some such existential paradigm as blackbird/thrush/starling. Note that it is still a single selection if the other members of the set happen not to be birds; possibilities are endless, but we might have blackbird/rabbit/old boot. By contrast, (332) projects a context of interaction in which both *black* and *bird* are selective. The existential paradigm might, for instance, be

	black	bird
It's a		
	brown	mammal

separate specification being required of colour and zoological classification. But it is easy to conceive of a context in which one or other can be taken to be specified already, and if it is bird that is already determined, the difference between (331) and (332) is neutralised:

(333) // but i ALways thought the <u>STAR</u>ling // was a <u>BLACK</u> bird //

---

(334) // <u>TOM</u> // WHAT do <u>YOU</u> think //

(335) // WHAT do <u>YOU</u> think tom //

In the kind of situation that comes most readily to mind for examples like these, we could say that in (334) *Tom* was selective in the sense that it nominates one of those present to give an opinion. In cases like (335) it will usually be safe to assume that the respondent has already been identified, perhaps by eye contact, before his name is mentioned: conversationalists do not often ask questions and *then* say who they want to answer them, so examples (334) and (335) illustrate a common difference in the intonational treatment of initial and non-initial vocatives. (Classroom procedure provides a notable exception of course: some teachers do make a point of identifying the respondent after the question has been put, as for instance in // WHO knows where TEA comes from // TOM //).

---

(336)   // i'm VERy TIRED //

(337)   // i'm NOT very TIRED //

The likelihood of there being a prominent syllable in *very* in (336) relates directly to the likelihood that it will represent an existential choice from, say, very/rather/slightly. The improbability of there being one in (337) relates to the fact that there would not normally be thought to be such a choice after the negative: 'I'm not rather/slightly tired' seems distinctly odd. The expectation of there being no selection in this slot is so strong that in an utterance like

(338)   // he's NOT too KEEN //

too will usually be interpreted as an existential synonym of *very*, having a quite different discourse value from that it has in:

(339)   // he's TOO KEEN //

---

(340)   Speaker A: // and it ALL HAP pened // at the DIFficult time
        of   LIFE //
        Speaker B: // well it was CERtainly A difficult time // YES //

Speaker A here projects an assumption that one particular time of life can be identified as the difficult one. Speaker B's assumptions prove, however, to be of a different kind: for him/her the choice between *a* and *the* is a crucial one in this particular context, and he/she draws attention to the existence of the choice in his/her response. The slight awkwardness about the unreduced vowel in *A* (and in any selective presentation of *the*) draws attention to the fact that it is unusual for either of the articles to represent a sense selection. Grammar may see them as in systematic opposition, but most occurrences in discourse are of one of two kinds:

(i)   There is no possibility of choice:
        What was the weather like?
        Isn't it a pity!

(ii)   There is a choice of words but no choice of sense:
        The rose is more colourful than the lily.
        A rose is more colourful than a lily.

What differentiates the last two is not so much the statements they make about the world, as *which* world is projected as the already-understood background against which the assertion is set. We can regard it as a stylistic choice, in the sense that it has to do with the linguistic conventions that go with present activity: gardeners and botanists, we may surmise, take it that they occupy a world in which *the* is the commonest choice, while *a* might serve to reify a complementary understanding shared by flower-arrangers.

High key

(341)   // they're reQUIRED // . . . // to TAKE these deCISions // on
        PA per //

(For the context of this fragment, see page 12.) The speaker is offering, as one reason why certain administrative decisions are unsatisfactory, the fact that the officials making them do not meet the interested parties in person. The existential opposition projected is between taking decisions *on paper* and taking them on the basis of an interview: 'face to face', as he/she says later. The assumption is that taking them on paper goes against the reasonable expectations of anyone who is interested in making the procedure more efficient.

---

(342)   Speaker A: // i THOUGHT you LIKED living in london //

        Speaker B: // i DO //

The second speaker's *I do* contradicts the assumption underlying what the first speaker says: 'It is *not* the case, as your remark seems to imply, that I don't. We can compare this contradictory response with the acquiescent mid-key response in:

(343) Speaker A: // i exPECT you LIKE living in london //
       Speaker B: // i DO //

We must beware of simplifying, however. There is a conversational use of high key in this kind of situation which serves to lend emphasis to the agreement.

---

(344) Speaker A: // whatEVer's the MATter //

       Speaker B: // the BOSS has been sacked //

On page 29, we considered the way the prominence system is exploited in this example. We can now see how the unexpectedness of the event is further emphasised by particularising use of high key. The meaning increments deriving from this combination of key choice and prominence distribution add up to something like: 'Who do you think has been sacked? The boss, rather than any of the people whose sacking you would regard as more likely' or, more colloquially, 'the boss of all people!'

---

(345) // AS for the SECond half of the game // it was UNbeLIEVable //

Double prominence indicating word quotation (see page 142) together with particularising use of high key often carries the implication 'of all the words I could use, the one I choose as the only one appropriate is . . .'. Contrastive word choice can only be distinguished from contrastive sense choice like this if the word in question has a syllable to carry the special prominence. In

(346) // AS for the SECond half of the game // it was MARvellous //

different situations might favour either of the interpretations: 'It was marvellous against expectations' (perhaps in the light of an earlier account of the first half); or 'The only word to describe it is *marvellous*'. Explicit word quotation, such as occurs for instance in lessons and lectures, makes frequent use of particularising high key:

(347) // and the WORD for this process // is ELecTROLysis //

Low key

(348) Host: This is Mary.
      Guest: Pleased to meet you.
      Host: // and THIS is <u>PET</u>er // mary's _{<u>HUS</u>band} //

When introducing a married couple who can be assumed to be recognisable as a married couple, the host is likely to mark the existential equivalence of *Peter* and *husband*. To present *husband* as merely selective with mid key would be to project a context of interaction in which Peter might have some other status. Notice that there is a potentially important distinction between (348) and the following version:

(349) // and THIS is her <u>HUS</u>band // _{<u>PET</u>er} //

It is a distinction we can capture in some such way as:

     '. . . and this is Peter, in other words her husband.'
     '. . . and this is her husband, in other words Peter.'

The first projects an assumption that although Peter's name may not be known, the circumstances in which he is introduced will make the fact that he is married to Mary self-evident (although the assumption may have no foundation in fact: it may be a tactful ploy). The assumption projected by the second version (which may equally well have no more than a diplomatic justification) is that once he is identified as Mary's husband, Peter's name will be known. There is a socially helpful implication that the equation, *Mary's husband = Peter*, is part of the already-shared understanding.

---

(350) // ONly a <u>SMALL</u> number of people // SOMEthing like <u>HALF</u> // ACtually turned <u>UP</u> //

(351) // ONly a <u>SMALL</u> number of people // _{SOMEthing like <u>HALF</u>} // ACtually turned <u>UP</u> //

In (350), the speaker judges it necessary to make clear what he/she means by a small number. In (351) his/her choice of low key for the second tone unit carries the implication that, for present purposes, *a small number* is understood to mean something like *half*.

---

(352) $||$ the SPEAKer was <u>ILL</u> $||$ so the LECture was <u>CAN</u>celled $||$

The example resembles (81) that we discussed earlier, except that the connective *so* makes the causal relationship explicit. We have seen that such a relationship is implicit in (81) and shall therefore expect that *so* will be non-prominent: since it duplicates information already present, it cannot be a sense selection. We could construct a similar alternative to (82) with a non-prominent *because* in the second tone unit.

Termination

(353) $|| p$ the <u>BOSS</u> has been sacked $||$

We have already seen how the contrastive value of high key and a special exploitation of the prominence system each contributes separate increments to the value of this utterance. We can now add that, because high termination is selected simultaneously with high key, the hearer is invited to respond 'actively'. An implied 'What do you think of that?' is a close paraphrase. Among the high-key responses that would satisfy the expectation of concord might be

(354) $|| p$ <u>REAL</u>ly $||$; $|| p$ <u>GOOD</u>ness $||$; $|| p$ <u>SACKED</u> $||$

and since each of these also has high termination, a high key, adjudicating $|| p$ <u>YES</u> $||$ would be an appropriate rejoinder. Notice that, since both key and termination are high in

(355) $|| p$ i CAN'T be<u>LIEVE</u> it $||$ and $|| p$ you DON'T <u>SAY</u> so $||$

either of these would also invite an adjudicating *yes*; but mid termination in otherwise similar utterances produces a quite different effect:

(356)   Speaker A: $|| p$ the <u>BOSS</u> has been sacked $||$

   Speaker B : $|| p$ i DON'T be<u>LIEVE</u> it $||$

---

(357) Speaker A: $||$ p i'm LEAVing on FRIday $||$

Speaker B: $||$ p $\underline{\text{LEAV}}$ing $||$

(358) Speaker A: $||$ p i'm LEAVing on FRIday $||$

Speaker B: $||$ p on $\underline{\text{FRI}}$day $||$

In both these cases, the second speaker disregards the expectation that he/she will respond in mid key. We may say that he/she takes an independent attitude with respect to A's news rather than passively admitting it to his/her view of things as A assumes he/she will. The responses have both high key and high termination: there are contrastive implications – *leaving* (not for example, staying), *Friday* (not when I expected you to leave); and also invitations to adjudicate – 'Did you say/ mean *leaving*, or *Friday*'. The following version loses the increment of contrast but retains the other increment:

(359) Speaker A: $||$ p i'm LEAVing on FRIday $||$

Speaker B: $||$ p LEAVing on $\underline{\text{FRI}}$day $||$

In practice, repetitions or part-repetitions that have high termination like these three are often interpreted rather differently. It can usually be taken as unlikely that the second speaker thinks he/she has misheard and simply wants his/her repetition evaluated. More often the first speaker will regard it as an invitation to expand in some way. Nevertheless, the expected high-key *yes* is likely to precede the expansion:

(360) Speaker B: $||$ p LEAVing on $\underline{\text{FRI}}$day $||$

Speaker A: $||$ p $\underline{\text{YES}}$ $||$ p i HAVE to be in $\underline{\text{LON}}$don $||$ r+ on SATurday $||$

---

(361) $||$ p that will be FORty- $\underline{\text{FIVE}}$ $||$ r+ $\underline{\text{PLEASE}}$ $||$

(362) $||$ p that will be FORty- $\underline{\text{FIVE}}$ $||$ r+ $\underline{\text{PLEASE}}$ $||$

This pair of examples illustrates one effect of a termination choice that does not come at the end of an utterance. In (361) the supermarket cashier states the price of the purchase and assumes concurrence. In (362) he/she does exactly the same except that the high termination invites adjudication. In neither case is the customer likely to respond audibly until after the subsequent, mid-termination, concurrence-expecting *please*. There is a marked difference in the effects, however, traceable to the fact that in the second, but not the first, there is a kind of ritual acknowledgment that the customer has had some part in arriving at the total.

---

(363) // p perHAPS you could <u>HELP</u> him //

(364) // p perHAPS you could <u>HELP</u> him //

The differential expectations of concurrence and adjudication in these two utterances would often result in the first having the local meaning of a 'suggestion' and in the second being interpreted locally as a 'question', the expected responses being *yes* (= 'perhaps I could' or 'what a good idea!') and adjudicating *yes* respectively. There is a somewhat similar difference between:

(365) // p i WONder if he'll <u>MAKE</u> it // and

(366) // p i WONder if he'll <u>MAKE</u> it //

The version with high termination would often be interpreted as 'Do you think he'll make it?' inviting either 'Yes I do (think)' or 'No, I don't (think)' instead of the 'Yes, so do I (wonder)' invited by the other version.

Referring tone

(367) Speaker A: Where do you do your shopping?
       Speaker B: // r <u>US</u>ually // p i <u>GO</u> to the <u>SUP</u>ermarket //

The question is unrestricted as to frequency: it could be said to include 'Where do you usually/always do your shopping?' and possibly others in its potential meanings. The respondent selects one of these to restrict the application of his/her answer: 'I presume you mean – that is to say I take it as negotiated common ground – that you mean where do I usually do it . . . ?'

(368) Speaker A: // When do you do your shopping?
       Speaker B: // r i <u>GO</u> to the <u>SUP</u>ermarket // p on <u>FRI</u>days //

In this case it is the inclusive term *shopping* that is analysed by the second speaker, who replies selectively with respect to that part of his/her shopping that is done at the supermarket.

(369) Speaker A: What did Peter say about it?
Speaker B: // p i DIDn't TELL // r HIM about it //

At first sight this might seem like a counter-example. *Him* seems to be a simple replacement for *Peter* and therefore non-selective. An alternative version

(370) // p i DIDn't TELL him about it //

would recognise this fact. To interpret B's contribution in (369) we have to recognise that he/she is doing rather more than answer the question he/she has been asked. Because the system is exploitable, he/she has the option of projecting a situation in which *him* is selective, even if by so doing he/she seems to be violating the discourse conditions as a dispassionate analyst might define them. What he/she does is to assume a world in which Peter was one of several who might have been told, and on this basis answers selectively.

(371) Speaker A: Her brother's a lawyer.
Speaker B: // r there are LAW yers // p and LAW yers //

The linking together of lexical items in this idiom would scarcely be conceivable if the otherwise identical selections were not differentiated intonationally. We can usefully compare this kind of linking with that which we find, for instance, in:

(372) // p the journey took HOURS // p and HOURS // (. . . p and HOURS)

Here, each proclaimed tone unit adds an additional expression of tedium to a cumulative chain. By contrast, (371) treats the word *lawyer* as the realisation of two senses. The existential sense paradigm projected is:

'lawyer' of one kind
'lawyer' of another kind

r+ and p+ tones

(373) Speaker A: Who was at the meeting last night?
Speaker B: // r+ there was PETer // r+ and MARy // r+
and   HENry //

Much of what we said about the intonation of counting applies also to lists: something that we can identify as a 'list' may occur in a wide variety of discourse conditions, and the tone choices will reflect those conditions in the same way as they do elsewhere. Example (373) projects a context of interaction in which the items listed are all members of a known set: the people referred to are selected from those whom the hearer will think are likely to have been at the meeting. If someone was there unexpectedly, or if there was someone there whom the hearer did not know, we can expect proclaiming tone:

(374) // r+ there was PETer // r+ and MARy // p and a MISter JONES //
p i DON'T think you've MET yet // r+ and HENry // . . .

Both (373) and (374) are open lists. A proclaiming tone serves to close a list, a fact we can relate directly to our comments on counting. A closed list, like

(375) // r+ there was PETer // r+ and HENry // p and MARy //

presents information about both who was there, and how many. It is because we think of the presenting of a list as a unified and uninter-rupted activity that we most easily associate the dominant version of the tone with it. If r tone is used, it is likely that the hearer will feel free to intervene between items:

(376) Speaker B: // r well there was PETer //
Speaker A: // r+ YES //
Speaker B: // r and MARy //
Speaker A: // p i WONdered whether // r+ SHE'D come // . . .

The choice of r+ tones in this last example marks Speaker A as unmistak-ably occupying dominant role, not the speaker presenting the list.

---

(377) // r PETer // . . . // r CAN you HEAR me //

(378) // r+ PETer // . . . // r+ CAN you HEAR me //

Referring tone is frequently used to get the attention of someone who is thought to be within earshot, in conjunction either with the person's name or some other locution. If a first attempt with r tone is unsuccessful, a repeated call with $r+$ tone adds dominance implications to the probable increase in loudness. There is a similar alternation of p tone and $p+$ tone in:

(379) $// p \underline{\text{PET}}\text{er} // \ldots // p \underline{\text{STOP}}$ it $//$

(380) $// p+ \underline{\text{PET}}\text{er} // \ldots // p+ \underline{\text{STOP}}$ it $//$

---

(381) $// r$ well the $\underline{\text{DIF}}$ficulty of course $// r$ if we WANT to under$\underline{\text{STAND}}$ the paper $// r+ \underline{\text{IS}} // r+ \underline{\text{THAT}} // \ldots$

In serious discussions of the seminar kind, speakers often begin a contribution by projecting a state of convergence. After the ritual accommodation to the view-point and to the assumed control of others with r tone, the change to $r+$ tone marks a characteristic assumption of dominant role. The change is the more noticeable because neither *is* nor *that* is likely to constitute a sense selection. Both have prominence for the sole purpose of carrying the tone selection and its social connotations. The speaker establishes himself/herself in the role of controller of the discourse for the time being, a role which resembles, in those respects that concern us at present, that of story-teller. The sense of deliberation and of careful choice of words which this kind of delivery can produce is exemplified in part of the extract we examined at the beginning of Chapter 1:

(382) $\ldots // p$ it's be$\underline{\text{CAUSE}} // r+$ they HAVEn't had the oppor$\underline{\text{TUN}}$ity $//$
   $// p$ of $\underline{\text{TALK}}$ing $// r+$ FACE to $\underline{\text{FACE}} // r+$ WITH the $\underline{\text{CLAIM}}$ant $//$
   $// r+$ and REALly $\underline{\text{FIND}}$ing $// p$ the $\underline{\text{FACTS}} //$

APPENDIX B

Fundamental frequency traces of some representative tone units

Objectivity is a highly desirable end in this as in all areas of linguistics, and the pursuit of objectivity is commonly associated nowadays with the increasingly sophisticated instrumentation that is becoming available. The argument has been developed, however, that the investigation of the physical correlates of the meaning-carrying categories is an entirely separate task, logically dependent on prior recognition of what these categories are. It is also likely, given the variables mentioned, to be a complex one. To give any account of physical correlates at this point, it is necessary to be clear that we are doing so under conditions where as many of these variables are controlled as is feasible. The set of fundamental frequency traces that follow were produced primarily with a view to demonstrating that each of the categories of the tone unit *is capable of being distinguished* on the basis of *pitch variation alone*. Apart from thus taking no account of other phonetic variables, they represent highly selective performances in each of the following respects:

  i they are all produced by one speaker (the author);
 ii they are spoken without any context;
iii they are recorded under studio conditions, and with the speaker being fully aware that he is producing a specimen of each of the phonological variables in turn.

Obviously, the results have to be approached with all these facts in mind. They have, however, been found useful in providing a rough guide to what we can expect to find when we come to examine naturally-occurring talk. They are included here in the hope that they will help readers without suggesting an inappropriate concern with the minutiae of physical realisation.

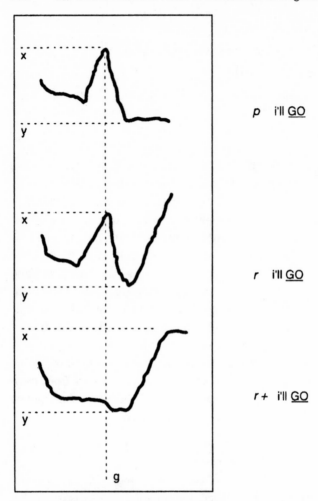

p i'll <u>GO</u>

r i'll <u>GO</u>

r+ i'll <u>GO</u>

The three frequently used tones with monosyllables
Level X determines *key* and/or *termination*.
Level Y, at which there is a change of steepness or direction, is roughly
constant for the speaker, as is the time interval XY.

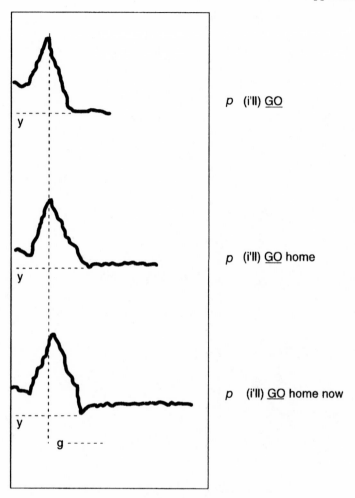

Enclitic segments following p tone (no interruption of voicing)
**The effect of adding an enclitic segment is principally to lengthen the
duration of the trace after the 'turn' at level Y.**

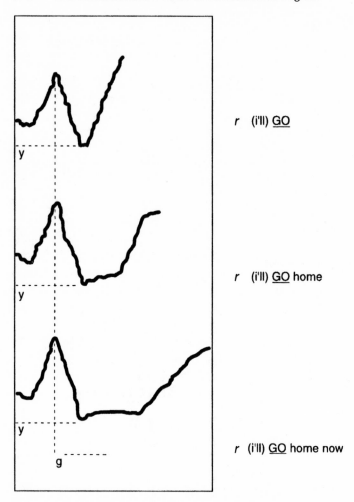

r (i'll) <u>GO</u>

r (i'll) <u>GO</u> home

r (i'll) <u>GO</u> home now

Enclitic segment following r *tone (no interruption of voicing)*
The trace is lengthened by a trough following the turn at level Y and by a decrease in the steepness of the final rise.

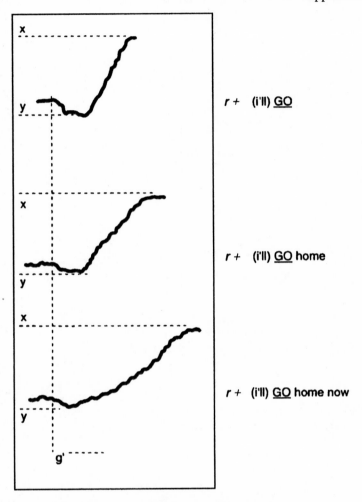

r + (i'll) <u>GO</u>

r + (i'll) <u>GO</u> home

r + (i'll) <u>GO</u> home now

Enclitic segment following r + *tone (no interruption of voicing)*
**Pitch level X is achieved at the end of the enclitic segment, the extra time
being taken up in the ascent from Y to X.**

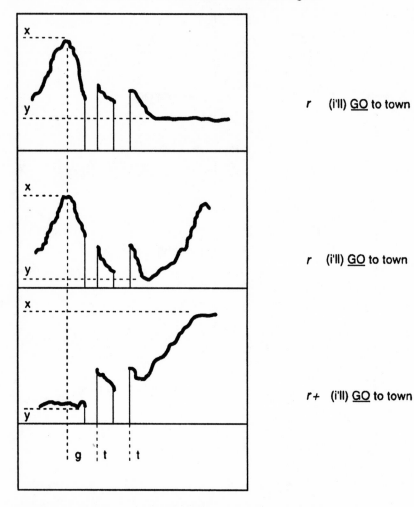

r   (i'll) <u>GO</u> to town

r   (i'll) <u>GO</u> to town

r+   (i'll) <u>GO</u> to town

Enclitic segments with interrupted voicing
Each resumption of voicing occurs at a higher pitch level than the simple
pattern of the tone would lead one to expect and is followed by a brief fall.
After *r* and *p* tones this increases the time taken to achieve level Y. After
r+ tone it results in the rise to level X having a saw-tooth appearance.

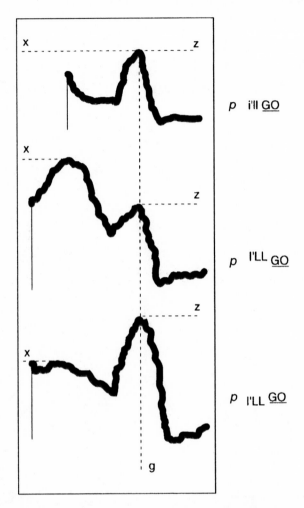

p i'll <u>GO</u>

p I'LL <u>GO</u>

p I'LL <u>GO</u>

Comparison of non-prominent with prominent monosyllables preceding tonic, with rise or fall between the resultant two prominent syllables. (Tone p)

Level X determines *key*; level Z determines *termination*.

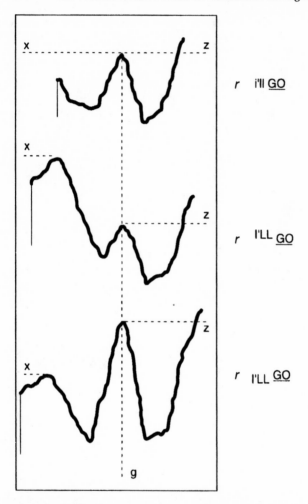

r i'll <u>GO</u>

r I'LL <u>GO</u>

r I'LL <u>GO</u>

Non-prominent and prominent syllables compared before r tone, showing effect of step up and step down between onset syllable and tonic syllable.
Level X determines *key*; level Z determines *termination*.

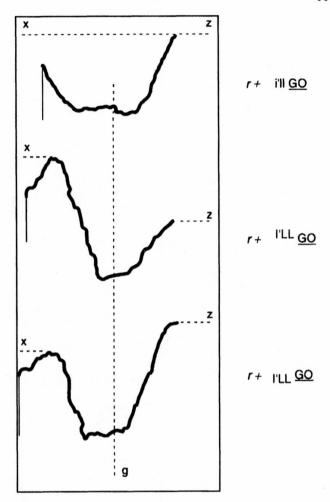

r + i'll <u>GO</u>

r + I'LL <u>GO</u>

r + I'LL <u>GO</u>

Non-prominent and prominent syllables compared before r + tone, showing effect of step up and step down between onset syllable and tonic syllable.

Level X determines *key*; level Z determines *termination*.

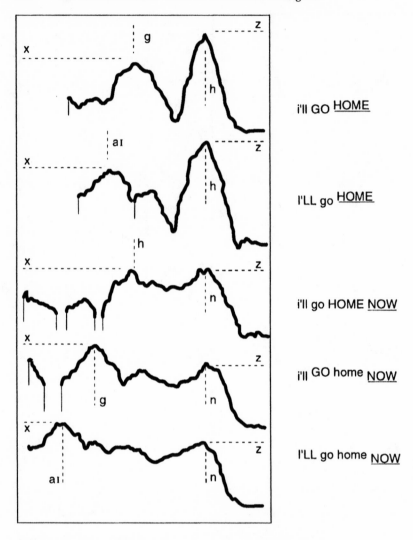

i'll GO <u>HOME</u>

I'LL go <u>HOME</u>

i'll go HOME <u>NOW</u>

i'll GO home <u>NOW</u>

I'LL go home <u>NOW</u>

Various combinations of prominent and non-prominent syllables before p *tone*

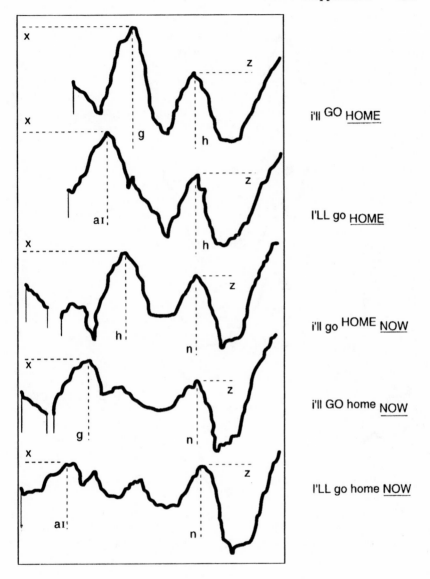

i'll GO <u>HOME</u>

I'LL go <u>HOME</u>

i'll go HOME <u>NOW</u>

i'll GO home <u>NOW</u>

I'LL go home <u>NOW</u>

Various combinations of prominent and non-prominent syllables before r tone

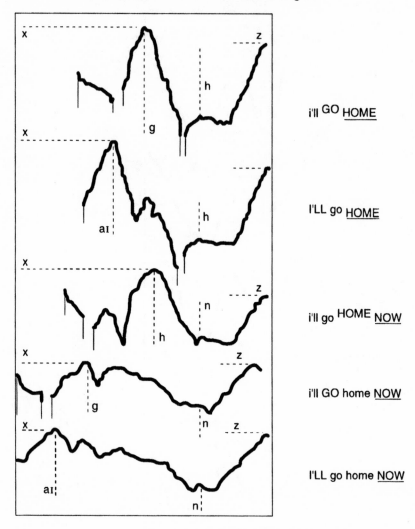

i'll ^{GO} <u>HOME</u>

I'LL go <u>HOME</u>

i'll go ^{HOME} <u>NOW</u>

i'll GO home <u>NOW</u>

I'LL go home <u>NOW</u>

Various combinations of prominent and non-prominent syllables before r + *tone.*

APPENDIX C

List of technical terms

additive (p. 124)
adjudication (p. 49)
concord (p. 54)
context of interaction (p. 25)
continuative (p. 88)
contrastive (p. 41)
direct orientation (p. 133)
dominant (p. 184)
enclitic segment (p. 13)
equative (p. 50)
existential equivalence (p. 50)
existential paradigm (p. 23)
existential sense (p. 33)
existential synonymy (p. 33)
exploitation (p. 27)
extended tonic segment (p. 14)
general paradigm (p. 23)
incompatible senses (p. 33)
internal key and termination
    choice (p. 122)
key (p. 11)
minimal tonic segment (p. 14)

oblique orientation (p. 133)
onset syllable (p. 10)
opposition (p. 1)
paradigmatic dimension (p. 22)
particularising (p. 45)
pitch sequence (p. 117)
P/R opposition (p. 69)
proclaiming tone (p. 69)
proclitic segment (p. 13)
projection (p. 27)
prominence (p. 7)
referring tone (p. 69)
selection (p. 21)
sense dimension (p. 32)
syntagmatic dimension (p. 22)
termination (p. 11)
tone (p. 9)
tone system (p. 9)
tone unit (p. 3)
tonic segment (p. 13)
tonic syllable (p. 9)

David Brazil bibliography

Brazil, D. (1969) Kinds of English: spoken, written, literary. *Educational Review*, 22/1, 78–92.

(1972) *An investigation of the relationship between intonation and grammar in the reading aloud of citation forms.* Unpublished masters dissertation. Birmingham: University of Birmingham.

(1975) *Discourse intonation: Discourse analysis monographs no. 1.* Birmingham: University of Birmingham, English Language Research.

(1976) The teacher's use of intonation. *Educational Review*, 28/3, 180–189.

(1978a) *Discourse intonation.* Unpublished doctoral dissertation. Birmingham: University of Birmingham.

(1978b) *Discourse intonation II: Discourse analysis monographs no. 2.* Birmingham: University of Birmingham, English Language Research.

(1978c) *Discourse intonation: supplement to the final report to SSRC for the period 1st September 1975 to 31st August 1978.* Birmingham: University of Birmingham, English Language Research.

(1981a) Discourse analysis as linguistics: A response to Hammersley. In P. French and M. Maclure (eds.) *Adult-child conversation* (59–72). London: Croom Helm.

(1981b) Intonation. In R. M. Coulthard and M. Montgomery (eds.) *Studies in discourse analysis* (39–50). London: Routledge & Kegan Paul.

(1981c) The place of intonation in a discourse model. In R. M. Coulthard and M. Montgomery (eds.) *Studies in discourse analysis* (146–157). London: Routledge & Kegan Paul.

(1982a) Impromptuness and Intonation. In N. E. Enkvist (ed.) *Impromptu Speech: A Symposium.* Publications of the Research Institute of the Åbo Akademi Foundation, No. 78, 277–289.

(1983a) Intonation and connectedness in discourse. In K. Ehlich and H. van Riemsdijk (eds.) *Connectedness in sentence, discourse and text: Proceedings of the Tilburg Conference held on 25 and 26 January 1982.*

Tilburg Studies in Language and Literature 4, (179–198). Le Tilburg: Tilburg University.

(1983b) Intonation and discourse: Some principles and procedures. *Text* 3/1, 39–70.

(1984a) Tag questions. *Ilha do Desterro: V/11*, 28–44.

(1984b) The intonation of sentences read aloud. In D. Gibbon and H. Richter (eds.) *Intonation, accent and rhythm: Studies in discourse phonology* (46–66). Berlin: Walter de Gruyter.

(1985a) *The communicative value of intonation in English.* Birmingham: University of Birmingham, English Language Research.

(1985b) Phonology: Intonation in Discourse. In T. A. van Dijk (ed.) *Handbook of Discourse Analysis: Volume 2 Dimensions of Discourse* (57–75). London: Academic Press.

(1985c) Where is the edge of language? *Semiotica, 56–3/4,* 371–88.

(1986a) Discourse Intonation. In J. Morley and A. Partington (eds.) *Spoken Discourse: Phonetics Theory and Practice. Laboratorio degli studi linguistici* 1986/1 (35–45). Universita di Camerino.

(1986b) Investigating the intonation of language learners. In M. Cling and J. Humbley (eds.) *Hommage a A.C. Gimson: 3ème Colloque d'Avril sur L'Anglais Oral* (121–39). Paris: Université Paris-Nord.

(1986c) Intonation and the study of dialect. *Annual Report of Dialectology (Hiroshima) 29,* 263–278.

(1987a) Intonation and the grammar of speech. In R. Steele and T. Threadgold (eds.) *Essays in honour of Michael Halliday* (145–59). Amsterdam: Benjamins.

(1987b) Representing Pronunciation. In J. McH. Sinclair (ed.) *Looking up: An account of the COBUILD project in lexical computing* (160–166). London: Collins COBUILD.

(1990) 'Oh What is that Sound': An exercise in metrical analysis. In *Linguistic Fiesta: Festschrift for Professor Hisao Kakehi's Sixtieth Birthday* (67–82). Tokyo: Kuroshio.

(1991) Discourse intonation: The teacher's talk. *The Journal of English Language Teaching (India), XXVI/5,* 179–186.

(1992) Listening to people reading: In R. M. Coulthard (ed.) *Advances in discourse analysis* (209–241). London: Routledge.

(1992) Speaking English or talking to people. *Focus on English (British High Commission Madras), 7/2–3,* 16–23.

(1993) Telling tales. In J. McH. Sinclair, M. Hoey and G. Fox (eds.)

Techniques of Description: Spoken and written discourse (154–169). London: Routledge.

(1994) *Pronunciation for advanced learners of English*. Cambridge: Cambridge University Press.

(1994) The nature of English conversation. *Sophia Linguistica, 37*, 1–56.

(1995) *A grammar of speech*. Oxford: Oxford University Press.

Co-authored works

Coulthard, R. M. and Brazil D. (1979) *Exchange structure: Discourse analysis monographs no. 5*. Birmingham: University of Birmingham, English Language Research.

Brazil, D., Coulthard, R. M. and Johns, C. (1980) *Discourse intonation and language teaching*. Harlow: Longman.

Coulthard, R. M., Brazil, D. and Johns, C. (1979) Reading intonation. In G. Graustein and A. Neubert (eds.) *Trends in English text linguistics. Linguistische Studien Reihe A Arbeitsberichte 55*, (29–42). Berlin: Akademie der Wissenschaften der DDR Zentralinstitut für Sprachwissenschaft.

Sinclair, J. McH. and Brazil, D. (1982b) *Teacher talk*. Oxford: Oxford University Press.

Festschrifts

Coulthard, R. M. (ed.) (1986) *Talking about text: studies presented to David Brazil on his retirement. Discourse analysis monographs no. 13.* Birmingham: University of Birmingham, English Language Research.

Coulthard, R. M. (ed.) (1987) *Discussing discourse: studies presented to David Brazil on his retirement. Discourse analysis monographs no. 14.* Birmingham: University of Birmingham, English Language Research.

Select bibliography

Bolinger, D. (1958) Intonation and Grammar. *Language Learning* 8, 31–117.

Bolinger, D. (1964) Around the edge of language: intonation. *Harvard Educational Review*, 3C, ii, 282–293.

Bolinger, D. (ed.) (1972) *Intonation*. Harmondsworth: Penguin.

Brown, G., Currie, K. and Kenworthy, J. (1980) *Questions of Intonation*. The Hague: Croom Helm.

Chomsky, N. and Halle, M. (1968) *The Sound Pattern of English*. Cambridge, Mass: M.I.T. Press.

Crystal, D. (1969) *Prosodic Systems and Intonation in English*. London: C.U.P.

Crystal, D. (1975) *The English Tone of Voice*. London: Edward Arnold.

Goldman Eisler, F. (1968) *Psycholinguistics: experiments in spontaneous speech*. Academic Press: London.

Halliday, M. A. K. (1961) Categories of the theory of grammar. In *Word* 17 (3) 241–92.

Halliday, M. A. K. (1967) *Intonation and Grammar in British English*. The Hague: Mouton.

Jefferson, G. (1972) Size sequences, in D. Sudnow (ed.), 294–338.

Malinowski, B. (1923) The problem of meaning in primitive languages in Ogden C. K. and Richards I. A. (eds.), 296–336.

O'Connor, J. D. and Arnold, G. F. (1973) *Intonation of Colloquial English*. London: Longman, 1961, Second Edition.

Ogden, C. K. and Richards, I. A. (1968) *The meaning of meaning*. London: Routledge & Kegan Paul, 8th edition.

Pike, K. L. (1945) *The Intonation of American English*. Ann Arbor: University of Michigan Press.

Sacks, H., Schegloff E. A. and Jefferson, G. (1974) A simplest systematics for the organisation of turn-taking for conversation. In *Language* 50(4), 696–735.

De Saussure, F. (1915) *Cours de linguistique générale*. Paris: Payot.

Schmerling, S. F. (1976) *Aspects of English Sentence Stress*. Austin and London: University of Texas Press.

Sinclair, J. McH. and Coulthard, R. M. (1975) *Towards an Analysis of Discourse*. London: O.U.P.

Sudnow, D. (ed.) *Studies in Social Interaction*. New York: The Free Press.

Printed in the United Kingdom
by Lightning Source UK Ltd.
102037UKS00002B/223-225